INDIANAPOLIS 500:

A Century of Excitement

Published by

Krause Publications, a division of F+W Media, Inc.
700 East State Street • Iola, WI 54990-0001
715-445-2214 • 888-457-2873
www.krausebooks.com

To order books or other products call toll-free 1-800-258-0929
or visit us online at www.krausebooks.com or www.Shop.Collect.com

Unless otherwise noted, the photographs in this book
are courtesy of the Indianapolis Motor Speedway archives.

Library of Congress Control Number: 2010925830

ISBN-13: 978-1-4402-1413-4
ISBN-10: 1-4402-1413-1

Cover Design by Rachael Knier
Designed by Shawn Williams, Heidi Zastrow
Edited by Dan Brownell

Printed in China

Writer Roger Huntington was in a wheelchair almost 30 years ago, when he paid a last visit to the Indianapolis Motor Speedway's Hall of Fame Museum. I was privileged to tag along as he rolled past the rows of racing machinery, stopping often to paint vivid word pictures about what made each one so special. It was an awesome lesson in the history of technology at Indianapolis, and an inspiration for this work.

The Indianapolis 500 is kaleidoscopic. We each see it a little differently. But the sights and sounds of the machines of the "500" and the characters who harnessed them are central to every view. They're what this book is about.

Many, many thanks to the Speedway organization, especially historian Donald Davidson and Ron McQueeney's photo department, for their help. Selecting just the right images from the millions in Speedway archives is a needle-in-the-haystack chore that would have been impossible without Mary Ellen Loscar's good-humored assistance. Special thanks to the Speedway licensing group, to Eric Powell and to Ellen Bireley's Hall of Fame Museum staff, especially Bill Spoerle and A.J. Fairbairn.

And thanks, also, to the volunteers who opened archives for me in the Allison museum at the Rolls-Royce Indianapolis facility.

Penske Racing's Pat Hozza and Kelby Krauss of Target Chip Ganassi helped clarify the whereabouts of some of the winning cars of the "500," and the wonderful people of the public libraries of Indianapolis and Detroit were generous with their time and counsel. I'm very grateful.

And like the multitudes who have been touched down through the years by the spectacle of the "500," I'd save a heartfelt thank-you for the Hulman/George family. One hundred years after its debut, 65 years after Tony Hulman bought the Speedway and saved the "500," the race remains the single largest one-day sporting event in the world and a motor sports phenomenon of the first order. Give the family an A+ in stewardship.

— Ralph Kramer

CONTENTS

HELIO CASTRONEVES: *A Dream Come True*

In 1996, when I first came to United States to race Indy Lights, I had many dreams, among them, Indianapolis. I had at that stage of my life almost ten years as a race car driver, five in Go Karts and four in open wheels in Brazil, South America and Europe. I came to America as a humble rookie, eager to learn, with stamina to overcome the challenges and, especially, seeing everything with optimism and faith.

One of these goals, no doubt, has always been racing at the Indianapolis Motor Speedway (IMS). I always dreamt that one day I would have the joy of participating in an Indy 500 race, on that wonderful oval track, full of tradition and in its centennial history had some of the best drivers in the world. At the beginning of the 1996 season, I was 20 years old and one of my dreams was that Indy 500. But the truth is that no matter how high I dreamed at that time, I could never imagine that Indianapolis would be part of my life in such a special way.

My relationship with Indianapolis goes back to 2000. The city is beautiful, its population receives me with great affection and I feel so good that I call it "my city, my hometown." I remember to this day the first time I walked into the Speedway; my heart beat stronger and I was amazed with all that structure, which I only knew through pictures or on television. Being at the track was already an incredible feeling; driving there was unbelievable. I was still discovering every inch of that sacred track, and with each lap I was happier because I was living the dream of being in Indianapolis. That was in August 2000 in a test performed immediately after the race in Michigan.

I could never imagine that in my first race I would win the Indy 500. It is very difficult to describe my emotions that day May 27, 2001. I had never experienced anything like this in my career. But if all this was much more than I had imagined, what about May 26, 2002, when I won for the second time at Indianapolis Motor Speedway? Indianapolis always brings me magical and unforgettable moments. I also had the chance to present my father with the second Indy 500 ring as a thank you for all the support he always gave me and keeps giving me so I can do what I love most in life, which is to be a race car driver.

In the following years victory did not come, but nonetheless it was exciting to be in Indianapolis, especially in 2003 when I came in second, behind my Penske teammate and close friend Gil de Ferran. But 2009 came and with it a whirlwind of feelings. My sister and I were coming from a victory in court, being fully acquitted of charges that we were accused of. Even though 2009 began as a sad and disturbing year it became later on, with the graces of God, one of the best years of my life. After all, on May 24, 2009 I won for the third time the biggest and the best race in the world – Indy 500! A victory that still is fresh in my memory and still brings me a lot of joy.

Because records are there to be broken, I started to look ahead and want intensely the fourth win and maybe to be part of a select group with the greatest drivers: AJ Foyt, Al Unser and Rick Mears. Several times I have been asked from journalists in the United States and Brazil: "If you had to choose between being Indycar champion and winning the Indy 500 for the fourth time, what would be your choice for 2010?" On all these occasions, while explaining that the championship is a goal that I have been trying very hard to achieve, the answer has always been this: "Winning the Indy 500 for the fourth time."

Undoubtedly, Indianapolis is part of my life and as long as God gives me the strength, I will be back every year at this track, trying to beat the records and to be deserving of the great affection of the public who every year comes to the Speedway.

Thanks Roger Penske! Since 2000 you have given me the ride and the best team to fight for another victory here in Indianapolis. Also, my warmest THANK YOU to the Hulman George family, who keep doing a fantastic job that allows us drivers to pursue ours dreams.

This book celebrates the centennial of Indianapolis and I am honored to be part of this history. When May 2011 comes, my destination will be the IMS and I will do the same in 2012, 2013, 2014, 2015 and many more years ahead! But don't think it will be any different than the 2000 test. When I arrive at 4790 West 16th Street surely my heart will beat faster!

— *Helio Castroneves*

DAVID LETTERMAN: *Memorial Day Memories*

Every Memorial Day when I was a kid, my family and I listened to the live broadcast of the Indianapolis 500. Everyone did—you could hear it all over the neighborhood. We could also hear the roar of the engines. We lived some distance to the east, and I suppose prevailing winds played a part. I saw the Speedway for the first time when we were driving by on a Sunday outing. To this day, the size is hard to fathom.

Jimmy Daywalt lived in my neighborhood, and we often walked to his house just to look at it. I met him when he brought a race car to my school, P.S. 55. He let us sit in the car. That is just about all a kid wants.

My first visit to the Speedway was for Sunday qualifying with my Uncle Earl. My family liked this idea because of the smaller crowd and lower ticket price. Once inside, regardless of what you see, the first thing you notice is the sound. The sound my uncle and I heard that day was a four-cylinder dirt car and its raucous echo. In those days, if you were trying to make the field on Sunday, chances are you were in a dirt car.

In 1956, when Pat Flaherty won the race, he flew to New York City the same day to be a guest on the television show What's My Line? I don't remember if the panelists identified his line, but I do remember the host, John Charles Daly, telling us that poor Pat was temporarily deaf from the roar of the race. I liked that.

Fans used to build scaffolding in the infield to sit on for a better view. In 1960 the whole mess came down, and several people were hurt or killed.

In 1955 I was climbing a tree in the front yard when I learned that Bill Vukovich died. In 1961 I was in eighth-grade gym class when I heard that Tony Bettenhausen died testing a car for Paul Russo. Many thought Tony Bettenhausen would be the first to break 150 mph in qualifying. I was on my front porch when I learned that Eddie Sachs and Dave MacDonald died. Sid Collins, the voice of the Indianapolis 500, was always the one to deliver the sad news.

In 1971 a local Dodge dealer supplied the pace cars. In return he got to drive the car that paces the start of the race. He came into the pits pretty hot, locked up the brakes, and plowed into some photographers.

I remember Rodger Ward, Sam Hanks, A.J. Foyt, Bobby Marshman, Troy Ruttman, Paul Goldsmith, Len Sutton, Jimmy Bryan, the Unsers (who had nine wins), Mario Andretti, Jack Brabham, Dan Gurney, Jim Clark, Jackie Stewart, Jochen Rindt, Graham Hill, and Masten Gregory (an American living in Paris). I saw Janet Guthrie, Lyn St. James, and Sarah Fisher. In 2005 I watched Danica Patrick finish fourth for Rahal Letterman Racing.

I wanted Mario to win more. I wished Lloyd Ruby, Roger McCluskey, Jim McElreath and Don Branson would win one. I remember two or three races that featured Jack Turner upside down on the main straight. I wanted Parnelli Jones and Joe Leonard to win in the turbine. I liked Dick and Jim Rathmann (I think they were each other). I liked the idea that they sold Corvettes to astronauts. Ray Harroun once bought me a sandwich.* I saw Jim Hurtubise, Rick Mears, Peter Revson, Swede Savage, Elmer George, Arnie Knepper, Emerson Fittipaldi, and Bill Cheesbourg. I liked Mark Donohue. He and Jim Clark died racing in Europe. The sport often takes its best. The Speedway has proven this many times. The loss of life, while devastating, has made the Indianapolis Motor Speedway hallowed ground and all the more meaningful to drivers and people like me.

In the 1970s, qualifying for the 500 and the Monaco Grand Prix were held on conflicting dates. Mario would fly all night to make it to both. Cool stuff like that doesn't happen these days. I saw Smokey Yunick's "Side Car" run and crash at the Speedway. I have recently seen photos of it, and it still looks like a bad idea. I saw the Novis, the Watsons, the Cooper-Climax, Colin Chapman, and the Lotus. I love that Dan Gurney thought Ford and Lotus would be a good idea.

In 1971 I was one of several announcers from WLWI channel 13 hired to cover the race for ABC. I was assigned turn 4. Early in the race Mario Andretti stepped out of his wrecked car and walked past me on his way to the pits. He was kind to stop and answer my idiot questions: "How's the track?" "How's the traffic?" "How's your sister?" And for the first time I was on network television.

In 1972 Sid Collins came to visit me at channel 13. We chatted in the announce booth, and he explained that he had many opportunities to work on shows for various networks in New York, but he had gotten so famous for being the voice of the Indianapolis 500 that he couldn't think of leaving. He told me I should try for something more than local broadcasting. He encouraged a dream I had shared with no one. Because of Sid Collins, I moved to Los Angeles in May 1975, hoping for a life in comedy. Bobby Unser won the race.

I met 500 winner Bobby Rahal in 1986. Bobby was one of the few guests on my television show to invite me to dinner. We became friends, then business partners, and in 2004 Buddy Rice won the Indianapolis 500 driving for Rahal Letterman Racing. I remember Bobby's son Graham, named for Graham Hill, running around the motor home when Bobby was racing. In May 2010 Graham drove for Rahal Letterman Racing in the 500. He finished a tough race in twelfth place.

Since my son Harry's birth I have tried to give him big and small, thoughtful and silly lessons and anecdotes from my life. Routinely I announce, "Ladies and gentlemen, now that he's got his helmet off, let's really let him hear it." Thank you, Tom Carnegie.

I know untold numbers of Hoosiers have stories about the Indianapolis 500 as a fixture in their lives. For me, it became a friend.

* This is not true

Mr. Letterman would like you to know that he commutes daily from Westchester County to New York City accompanied by a riding mechanic. **

In 1967, on a dare, Mr. Letterman ate a tire. ***

Further, Mr. Letterman would like you to know that in 1983 he was beaten senseless by Teo Fabi. ****

** This is not true.

*** This is also not true.

****This is true.

— *David Letterman*

Ray Harroun and Marmon Wasp
in 1911 pre-race photo.

100 years after this Marmon race car won the first Indianapolis 500, the snowy winter scene at the Speedway adds perspective and a certain timeless cachet.

A STROKE OF GENIUS
1911-1919

❝ We're talking about the greatest automobile race ever put on anywhere on the face of the earth. Everything connected with it is going to have to be bigger and better than ever before—or we'll miss the boat. ❞

— Carl Fisher, 1910

The defining moment occurred September 4, 1910, the last day of the last racing weekend of what had become a losing year at the Indianapolis Motor Speedway. That's when Carl Fisher and his partners, Jim Allison, Art Newby, and Frank Wheeler, looked upon the 15,000 people scattered in the vast emptiness of their spacious palace and saw…unimaginable opportunity.

In the few months since the enormous track had been carved out of 320 acres of farmland just west of Indiana's capital city, the Fisher group had offered a smorgasbord of speed contests.

Theodore Myers

In 1910, young Theodore Myers was a partner in Carl Fisher's real estate agency. Asked to help with ticket sales, Myers was quickly so involved with Speedway business that he was hired full time. Soon, "Pop" Myers (so-named because of his prematurely white hair) was made general manager. For much of the next 40 years, through ownership changes, wars, and other assorted crises, he was the public face of the Speedway in Indianapolis.

There was something for almost everybody: motorcycles, airplanes, automobiles, and gas-filled balloons four stories high.

Fisher had declared again and again his objective in building the speedway was to provide Indianapolis carmakers, of which there were many in the first quarter of the 20th Century, a place to test and improve their products. But high board fences and huge grandstands going up, as the 2-1/2-mile rectangular strip of hardpack was going in, left no doubt there was another objective. Carl's proving ground was actually an enormous theater. He was in the entertainment business.

Sixty thousand spectators had witnessed the gruesome first round of auto races in 1909. There had been wrecks, injuries, even death. Then followed an emergency $400,000 re-paving (3.2

Jean Chassagne flipped his Sunbeam into the tall grass inside Turn 4 during the 1914 race.

million bricks at 13 cents apiece) that left the Fisher group's start-up budget in tatters.

A three-day Memorial Day kick-off to the 1910 season brought another 60,000 people through the gates. The partners breathed easier. But as the summer of '10 wore on, attendance dwindled. One July race day found less than 5,000 in the stands, after which Fisher ordered the cancellation of a scheduled August meet.

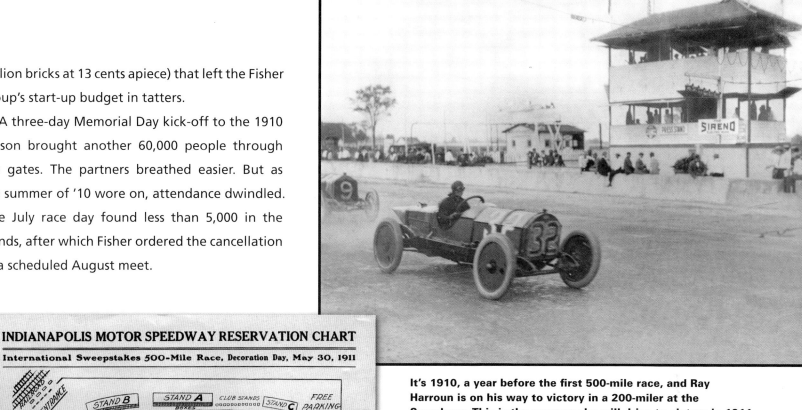

It's 1910, a year before the first 500-mile race, and Ray Harroun is on his way to victory in a 200-miler at the Speedway. This is the same car he will drive to victory in 1911.

INDIANAPOLIS MOTOR SPEEDWAY RESERVATION CHART

International Sweepstakes 500-Mile Race, Decoration Day, May 30, 1911

(hand-drawn track map labeled) RAILROAD · MAIN ENTRANCE · STAND B · STAND A · CLUB STANDS · STAND C · FREE PARKING SPACE · BOXES · PITS · WIRE · PITS · FREE PARKING SPACE · FIELD GATE · SCORE BOARD · JUDGES · SCORE BOARD · RESERVED AUTO PARKING SPACE · STAND D · FREE PARKING SPACE · SCORE BOARD · *Indianapolis Motor Speedway*

RACE STARTS AT 10 A. M. SHARP

General Admission at Main Entrance . $1.00   General Admission at Field Gate . 50 cents

MAIN ENTRANCE STANDS A—B—C   FIELD GATE STAND D

Seat Prices are in Addition to General Admission Charges

Boxes—Six Seats to Each Box—(In addition to $1.00 admission for each person)	$24.00
Single Box Seats—(In addition to $1.00 admission)	4.00
Club Stands—Seating 20 Persons—(In addition to $1.00 admission for each person)	50.00
Seats In Stand A—(In addition to $1.00 admission)	1.50
Seats In Stand B—(In addition to $1.00 admission)	1.00
Seats In Stand D—(In addition to 50 cents admission) Seats in Stand D are not reserved.	.50
Seats In Stand C—(In addition to $1.00 admission) Seats in Stand C are not reserved.	Free
Parking Space—Charge is in addition to general admission. Reserved Parking Space, per automobile	$2.00
All other parking space is free.	

Remittance Must Accompany All Reservations

Reservations will be filled in the order received.
The Speedway management reserves the right to reject any reservation and refund all money paid on same.
If the seats specified in any reservation order have been sold before receipt of that order, the Speedway management assumes the right to assign other seats as near as possible to those desired, unless return of remittance is requested in such event at time order is placed.
Patrons should specify first, second and third choice in seats when making reservations.
Tickets will be forwarded to purchaser as soon as reservation has been made. It is important that a correct address be furnished by each purchaser as no responsibility for loss of tickets in mail will be assumed by the Speedway management.

Make all checks, drafts and money orders payable to J. A. Allison, Secretary, Indianapolis Motor Speedway, Indianapolis, Ind.

Hand-drawn track map graces a flyer advertising the 1911 race.

A Stoddard-Dayton similar to the car Carl Fisher is driving around his unfinished track in 1909 will pace the first Indianapolis 500 in 1911.

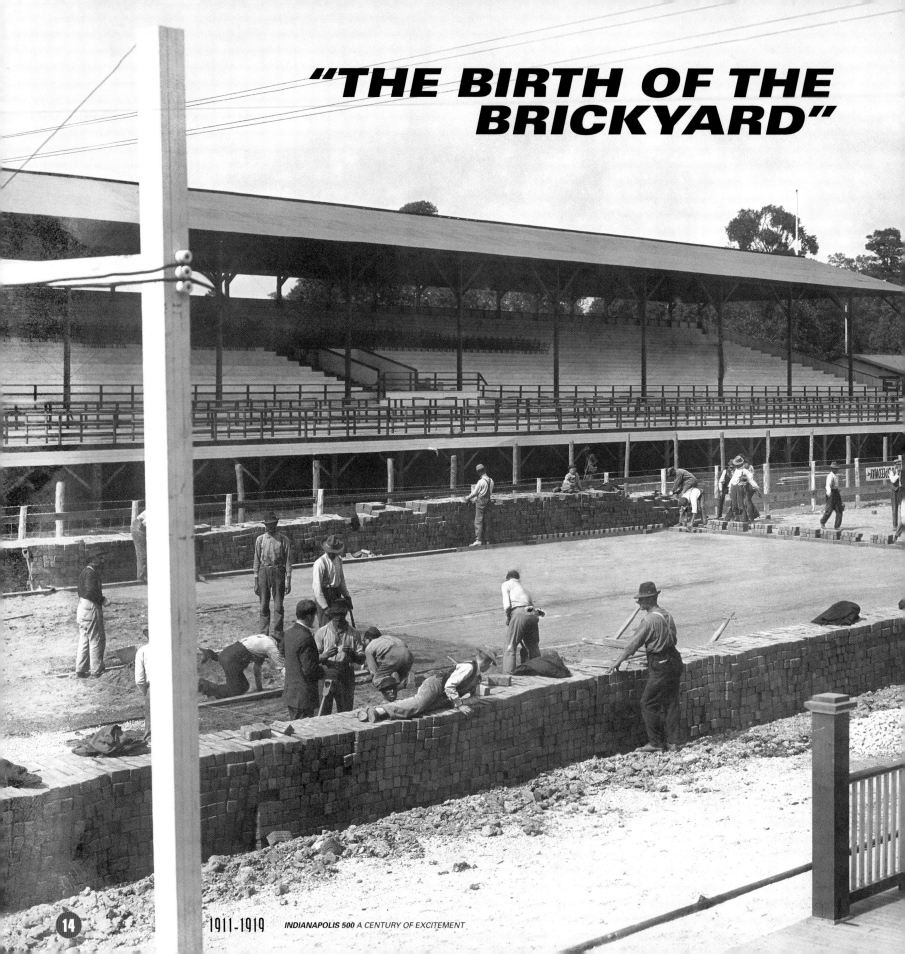

"THE BIRTH OF THE BRICKYARD"

Working small sections at a time, bricklayers took only 63 days in late 1909 to cover an inadequate crushed stone-and-tar surface with 3.2 million paving bricks. Forevermore, the Speedway will be known by millions of race fans around the world as *The Brickyard*.

Carefully stacked bricks await paving crews in Turn 1.

Paving instructions included how to build those slurry tables.

A steam-powered roller works a corner.

Louis Chevrolet was involved with Billy Durant and the founding of the Chevrolet Motor Co. in 1911; the first "500" where he appears as an entrant was in 1915. His radical little car was the "Cornelian." Of monocoque construction, it was powered by a 103 cid Sterling engine. Chevrolet started 23rd and dropped out after 76 laps.

Now, it was September 4, Labor Day, the season's grand finale. And one more time, spectators stayed away in droves.

From what's been said about how Fisher loved a challenge, the scene surely got his adrenaline pumping. The grade school dropout whose bicycle and automobile marketing stunts were legendary, who turned a mangrove swamp into Miami Beach, who would make millions and die poor, was likely brainstorming with his partners even before the Speedway's gates were closed that night.

Motor racing history was about to be made.

Just three days later, September 7, 1910, the Speedway broke the news that there would be a 500-mile race on Memorial Day, 1911. Since that was twice the length of any previous Speedway race, it got quite a bit of attention.

But Fisher wasn't done. Because of what else was announced, the Indianapolis 500 has been for 100 years the premier auto race in the world and the Indianapolis Motor Speedway the planet's most renowned auto racing institution.

First, competition at the Speedway would be limited to just this one event per year. No more smorgasbords. And second, the purse for 1911 would be $25,000, 10 times more than for any auto race before it. It would grow to $27,500 by race time, with $14,000 going to the winner.

The delicious combination of rarity and richness had the desired effect. The promise of a stupendous payday attracted big name drivers and carmakers from far and wide, which heightened public interest, which led to ticket sales.

As Memorial Day dawned Tuesday, May 30, 1911, Indianapolis was, indeed, the center of the motor racing universe. By train and car, by buggy, bicycle and on foot, pilgrims descended upon

PROFILE

Johnny Aitken

Johnny Aitken, an unsung hero of the Speedway's earliest days, was the first leader of the first "500." He managed the three-car National factory team in 1912. Asked to be something like a concierge to the European entries in 1913, he did the job so well that even more teams came over in 1914.

the city. Traffic gridlocked downtown. For miles around, hotels and rooming houses overflowed.

By mid-morning, the horde was encamped inside the Speedway five miles northwest of downtown. The newspapers said 80,000 people were on hand that day.

To the delight of many, a local boy named Ray Harroun, with relief from Cyrus Paschke, kept his sleek yellow Marmon racer out of trouble for almost seven hours on the way to winning the first 500. His average speed: 74.602 miles per hour.

For most of the next century, the formula remained the same. One race a year plus a pool of prize money that got bigger and bigger made the Indianapolis 500 more than just the

Frenchman Rene Thomas led a strong European contingent in 1914.

A Stoddard-Dayton like this paced the 1914 race.

Leather cap, face sock, and goggles were standard driver attire in the early days.

unquestioned main event in motorsport. The "500" became the standard, the star by which auto racing set its course.

If the 1911 payout was impressive, the $50,000 purse in 1912 was unbelievable.

This was the year teammates Joe Dawson and Howdy Wilcox, both driving Nationals, figured Mercedes driver Ralph DePalma was the man to beat. So Wilcox became the rabbit, pushing DePalma to drive harder than he planned. When DePalma's engine failed with two laps to go, Dawson made up a five-lap deficit to win the race

and $35,000. Drivers working together to achieve a team objective is not a recent phenomenon.

The Europeans arrived in 1913, albeit reluctantly. They reasoned if the pot of gold seemed too big to be true, it probably was. Finally persuaded by Fisher agents C.W. Sedwick and W.F. Bradley, teams from Peugeot, Sunbeam, and Isotta Fraschini gave the '13 race an international cachet. Mercedes was there, too, but the cars were privately owned.

The papers said 100,000 people watched Frenchman Jules Goux usher a Peugeot to a 13-minute victory, sipping champagne during pit stops along the way.

What was most intriguing about the Peugeot was its exquisite four-cylinder dual overhead camshaft engine. Copies began showing up quickly. Historians generally agree the venerable Offenhauser that would reign at Indianapolis for 40 years had its roots in the 1913 Peugeot.

Another big crowd watched the French run rampant in 1914, when the best an American team could do was fifth. That was Barney Oldfield in a Stutz.

Fred Wagner was the official starter at the Speedway from 1909 through '12. He did free-

1911 program.

First in a long line of flamboyant flagmen at the "500," Fred "Pop" Wagner posed with the checkered flag circa 1911.

1912 ticket.

1915 ticket.

1916 ticket.

The 1915 Packard pace car.

lance writing on the side, and his article on the 1913 race for *House Beautiful* magazine was caustic. "The reason why the American cars made a poor showing was obvious to anyone who visited the racing camps a day or two before the race," he said. "The foreigners were prepared and the Americans were not.

"Manufacturers who believe in exploiting their product by racing...must go to work and build out-and-out racers from the very start. All of the foreign racers were quite different from the stock models made by their respective manufacturers.

"The whole matter is analogous to trying to make a racehorse out of a brewery truck Percheron by a process of grooming and manicuring. It cannot be done."

Soon, war clouds darkened Europe. The Americans would again have the "500" largely to themselves, but a looming shortage of competitive entries at Indianapolis bothered Fisher and his partners.

Theodore E. "Pop" Myers, who began working at the track in 1910 and would stay until his death more than 40 years later, was asked in 1952 what they did about it. He told an interviewer that Fisher and Jim Allison decided to stock up on some race cars. They formed the Indianapolis Motor Speedway Team Co. and purchased two Peugeots.

Myers said track operators owning race cars was a dubious business practice, so the "situation" was not publicized.

"Arrangements were also made with the Maxwell Motor Car Co. for the lease of four

It's 1915, and hard-luck Ralph DePalma finally has a "500" victory.

A view of the area behind the timing and scoring buildings at the first Indianapolis 500 in 1911.

special Maxwells. In addition, the IMS team procured three Premier specials with engines designed and manufactured almost identical and exactly the cubic inch displacement size of the Peugeots."

To manage the team, they hired Eddie Rickenbacker, an energetic young driver from Columbus, Ohio. In 1927, he would buy the track.

As America teetered on the edge of World War I, the Speedway partners decided an autumn day of racing in 1916 might provide

Slow camera shutters in 1911 make speeding race cars into rakish works of art.

"EVOLUTION OF THE 500"

From the early 20th Century to the early 21st, almost everything about the "500" except the geography has changed greatly. The racecourse is still 2-1/2 miles around.

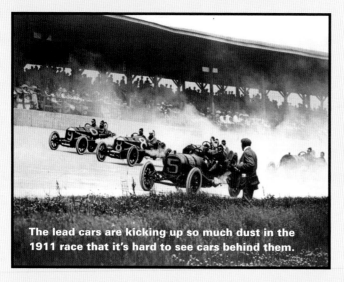

The lead cars are kicking up so much dust in the 1911 race that it's hard to see cars behind them.

In 1956 there's less dust, bigger crowds, and faster cars.

Modern Indy 500 races feature a state-of-the-art track, cars with advanced aerodynamics, and a world-wide television audience.

a little financial cushion against the expected dry spell ahead. The day consisted of three races, with Johnny Aitken winning all three in one of the Speedway cars. Gate receipts barely covered expenses (only 10,000 people showed up) but since six of the 16 cars in the field were

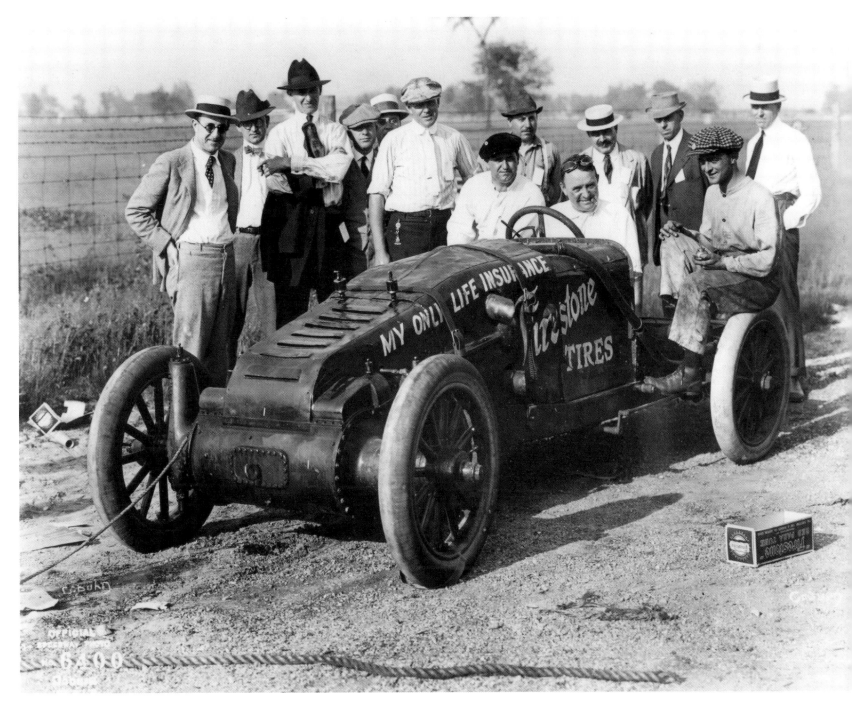

Barney Oldfield turned the first 100-plus mph lap at the Speedway in a pre-race exhibition in 1916 using his famous front-drive Christie. That's Barney behind the wheel. And yes, his signature cigar is in place.

This chain-reaction crash near the start/finish line in 1911 disrupted the scoring process.

Speedway property, the track paid itself almost half the $12,000 purse.

There was no racing at the track in 1917 and '18, as the facility was turned into a military airfield.

Rickenbacker, now a war hero, was what they called the "guest referee" when racing resumed in 1919. On a lark, he agreed to lend his name to a ghost-written account of the race.

Ace publicist Christy Walsh did the write-up. Rickenbacker gave it a fast read, and off it went via Western Union. Thirty-seven newspapers picked it up. They paid Rickenbacker $874, which he split with Walsh.

For winning the "500" (in a Speedway-owned Peugeot) Howdy Wilcox's cut of a $55,275 purse was $20,000.

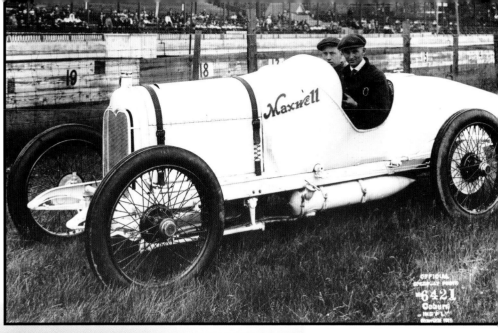

Seven cars in the abbreviated 1916 race were Speedway property. This was one. Pete Henderson, with relief from Eddie Rickenbacker, finished sixth.

Posed for a pre-race photo in 1919, Elmer Shannon's No. 23 Duesenberg looks good. But what catches the eye is the fellow on the utility pole in the background.

Illustration courtesy of David Kimble.

This exquisite David Kimble cutaway celebrates the jewel-like quality of one of Harry Miller's most famous race cars. Equipped with a radical intercooled centrifugal supercharger and running on pure methanol, it delivered a 124.02 mph one-lap record in 1928 that stood for nine years. Leon Duray was driving. The car is the property of the Speedway's Hall of Fame Museum.

THE ROARING '20s
1920-1929

▮▮There were two great clearinghouses of ideas concerning racing technology in those days. Miller in the west and Duesenberg in the east. They were the targets, and practically the only ones, for all of the good and bad ideas of the entire racing fraternity.▮▮

— Dick Loynes, 1933

The decade of the '20s at the Speedway started out with a bang and ended with a whimper. And the rollercoaster years in between saw massive rule changes, marvelously innovative machinery, a ticklish political imbroglio, new ownership, and ever bigger and more boisterous throngs making their annual pilgrimage to the corner of 16th Street and Georgetown Road.

Louis Chevrolet

Louis Chevrolet was the gifted son of a Swiss watchmaker. His skill in fixing things led him into auto racing. He won big races, built great race cars. His indomitable never-give-up spirit endured ill fortune and business failure. A grotto in his honor is a "must visit" feature outside the Hall of Fame Museum.

Auto racing around the U.S. had changed greatly in the teens. At first a pastime of the sporting set, it evolved into a ferocious test of guts and skill as it migrated from open roads to fairground horse tracks and hippodromes. It produced a new breed of daredevil driver, a warrior whose livelihood depended solely on his success on the track and the size of the purse. If the money was there, he went where gentlemen dared not.

For awhile at Indianapolis, everyone coexisted. But as the purse was augmented with high-dollar accessory awards, and mainstream carmakers took their cars and their employee/drivers out of the picture, the warriors became, with a few exceptions, the last men standing.

With the advent in 1920 of the $100 lap prize, the evolution became a revolution. First place at Indianapolis paid $20,000 at the time. Then, on top of thousands in accessory awards, you could collect *another* $20,000 if you led every lap. Or if your car was fast but fragile, you charged to the front and stayed there until it broke. And maybe you had yourself a pretty nice payday, anyhow.

In the 1925 race, this Duesenberg pace car was driven by Eddie Rickenbacker.

PHOTOS OF RACE DRIVERS
ENTERED IN THE 1922 500 MILE RACE.

PHOTO #2209 BY KIRKPATRICK COPYRIGHT-1922

DRIVER. E.G. "CANNON BALL" BAKER. MECH. SHORTY HANSON. CAR. FRONTENAC.

The cockpit of a two-man Indianapolis 500 car was a cozy place in 1922. The passenger seatback was slightly offset to the rear, which, in his case, put driver E.G. "Cannonball" Baker's right shoulder into the chin of his riding mechanic.

The Duesenberg brothers, Augie, left, and Fred, right, built race cars before they got into passenger car manufacturing.

Detroit Special Motor 500 Mile Race 1927.

With a lot of help from General Motors, this engine was built for Tommy Milton in 1927. Featuring a two-stage inter-cooled centrifugal supercharger, it powered the Detroit Special. The car was constructed in the Hyatt Bearings shop in the basement of the GM Building.

Dave Lewis' front-wheel drive 1926 car displays the exquisite craftsmanship that was a Harry Miller hallmark. The wire mesh was soldered together wire by wire.

Stripped of its bodywork, here's a typical Miller engine layout in the late '20s. Notice the huge supercharger.

"TIMING AND SCORING"

Early-day timing and scoring functions for the "500" seemed haphazard, but they did the job.

When the 1914 race was over, here's how one of the Speedway's huge scoreboards told the story.

Below: Just to the right of the adding machine is an 1876 ship chronometer, which was the critical component in a timing system Chester Ricker (standing) installed for the 1913 "500." It lasted through the '60s.

For years, volunteers wearing numbers matched to cars would move up and down a row of seats in the press area during the "500," keeping reporters apprised of the running order.

There's no evidence that the idea had been tried anyplace before Eloise "Dolly" Dallenbach, Theodore "Pop" Myers' assistant at the Speedway for 40 years, thought of it. But what the lap fund did was transform racing strategies. It kicked the level of combat up a few notches, which vastly intensified the drama for the breathless throngs swarming the grounds and grandstands. It was another stroke of genius, all the more so because the money came not from Speedway coffers but from Indianapolis residents and businesses that proudly "bought" a lap or two or more.

Given the aggressive nature of post-war auto racing in the U.S., and as American car builders like Harry Miller and the Chevrolet and Duesenberg brothers began producing really world-class machinery, the Europeans found the Indianapolis 500 no longer a cake walk. It would be 40 years before they would again take a checkered flag at Indianapolis.

That's not at all what Speedway management wanted to see happen. The international character of the "500" was not just accepted fact. It was central to the Speedway's unique allure. Through most of the teens, there had been almost as many foreign cars on the grid as there were U.S.-designed cars. More often than not, they were heavy crowd favorites.

When Indianapolis adopted in 1920 the same three-liter engine rule that Europe's Grand Prix road racing circuit was using, the goal was to encourage, not discourage, overseas participation. And two French companies, Ballot and Peugeot, did send teams.

Ralph DePalma, who had suffered the heart-breaking loss in 1912 when the engine in his Mercedes let go on the 198th lap, had one of the new eight-cylinder Ballots on the pole in 1920 at a

INDY PROFILE

Harry Miller

It is said eccentric Harry Miller got the ideas, Leo Goosen turned them into drawings, and Fred Offenhauser made them work. A Wisconsin native, Miller drifted finally to Los Angeles, where he opened a machine shop. He built carburetors, then engines and, eventually, entire race cars. His expensive jewel-like machinery dominated Indianapolis through the '20s and early '30s.

tick under 100 miles an hour. Again the race leader, he was stranded on the track with a magneto malfunction when Louis Chevrolet's young brother, Gaston, passed him on the way to victory.

As evidence of the distance the locals had come in race car engineering, the twin-cam four-cylinder engine in Chevrolet's winning Monroe was every bit as sophisticated as what the French came with. And the Monroe wasn't alone. Four Duesenbergs with new eight-cylinder engines were prepared for the race.

In 1921, Chevrolet's even more advanced Frontenac racer, this time powered by an aluminum straight-eight, would raise the bar again. Milton put it in Victory Lane after DePalma lost a connecting rod in his Ballot. And yes, he was leading at the time.

The back-to-back Indy wins brought even more fame to the Chevrolet brothers and their lightweight, high-tech Frontenac racers. But in another of the many cruel twists of fate visited upon the Chevrolets, a plan to capitalize on their

INDY PROFILE

Eddie Rickenbacker

Eddie Rickenbacker was a race driver long before he was a WW I flying ace. Then he was a General Motors sales executive. In Indianapolis in 1927 with an offer to buy Jim Allison's company, he was told it wasn't for sale, but the Speedway was. Soon, he had raised $750,000, and the track was his. He kept the Speedway going through the Great Depression, saw to its moth-balling during World War II, and sold it in 1945 for just what he paid for it.

L.L.Corum finished 5th in the '23 race in this Model T Ford speedster. Fitted with one of the Chevrolet brothers' special "Fronty" cylinder heads, it could run about 100 mph all day. Corum pitted only once and never changed tires.

This image of the Speedway on Race Day, 1922, is the one of oldest known aerial photos of the track. Looking southwest toward Turn 1 as the race apparently is about to start, it suggests, among other things, a certain casualness in the matter of spectator parking.

OFFICIAL PROGRAM
INDIANAPOLIS
MOTOR
SPEEDWAY

500

MONDAY - MAY - 31 - 1920
PRICE 15¢

1920 program.

The 1926 Chrysler Imperial 80 pace car.

Indy success triggered a financial setback from which the brothers would never fully recover.

Only a decade had passed since the short-lived partnership with Billy Durant had cost Louis the commercial rights to his name and a fortune in Chevrolet Motor Co. stock. Gaston had died in a West coast race not long after his "500" win.

Ohio investors persuaded Louis and Art to build a sporty little Frontenac production car. Incorporation papers were signed, a factory bought,

1929 ticket.

1926 ticket.

1920 ticket.

WINNER.
DRIVER. TOMMY MILTON
CAR. H.C.S. SPECIAL.
500 MILE RACE 1923.
INDIANAPOLIS MOTOR SPEEDWAY.

4325
KIRKPATRICK
419 W. WASH. ST.
INDPLS. IND.

After the forced liquidation of his holdings in the Stutz Motor Car Co., Harry Stutz entered this Miller-powered car for Tommy Milton to drive in the '23 Indy. Milton's first-place finish made him the first two-time "500" winner and the H.C.S. team $28,500 richer.

With superchargers soon to be banned, engine builders went all out in 1929 to deliver the ultimate package. That's a huge Roots-type blower suspended from the rear of this Delage engine.

Peter DePaolo

Peter DePaolo, one of Indy's most astute and entertaining personalities, was his uncle Ralph DePalma's riding mechanic in the early '20s. By 1925, he was lead driver of the Duesenberg factory team. His win that year came despite severely blistered hands that required a relief driver. His 1937 autobiography, *Wall Smacker*, is a delightful read.

and 1,500 workmen lined up. When a late 1922 Wall Street collapse sent their backers scurrying, the Chevrolets were left holding the bag. Louis filed a bankruptcy petition April 16, 1923.

Meanwhile, Indy was genuflecting to the Duesenbergs and an eccentric Californian named Harry Miller.

Fred and Augie Duesenberg had been building race cars since 1912. Neither were trained engineers, but it seemed Augie could make whatever Fred could design. They had built airplane engines, then race engines, then complete race cars, and the Duesenberg line of fine passenger cars that collectors covet to this day.

A Duesenberg finished second to Dario Resta in the 1916 "500." But what made Duesey a household word around the world was Jimmy Murphy's surprise rout of the best racing machinery Europe had to offer in the 1921 French Grand Prix. Fred had sent over a multi-car team. His secret weapon was a four-wheel hydraulic braking system. It was terribly erratic until Augie got the front-to-rear balance right, then the Dueseys could scream deeper into the curves and corners than the Ballots, Fiats and Sunbeams. Murphy won by 15 minutes. Race organizers were apoplectic.

Soon thereafter, Murphy bought the car, which he drove to victory in the 1922 "500." Along the way, he quietly swapped its engine for a new straight eight from a relatively unknown California shop owned by none other than Harry Miller. The engine was unquestionably a synthesis of the best design from Peugeot, Ballot, and, especially,

Duesenberg, including a sensational camshaft the Duesenbergs thought was theirs exclusively.

It made Harry Miller an auto racing superstar.

Murphy went on to win the 1922 AAA National Championship. Miller's shop was

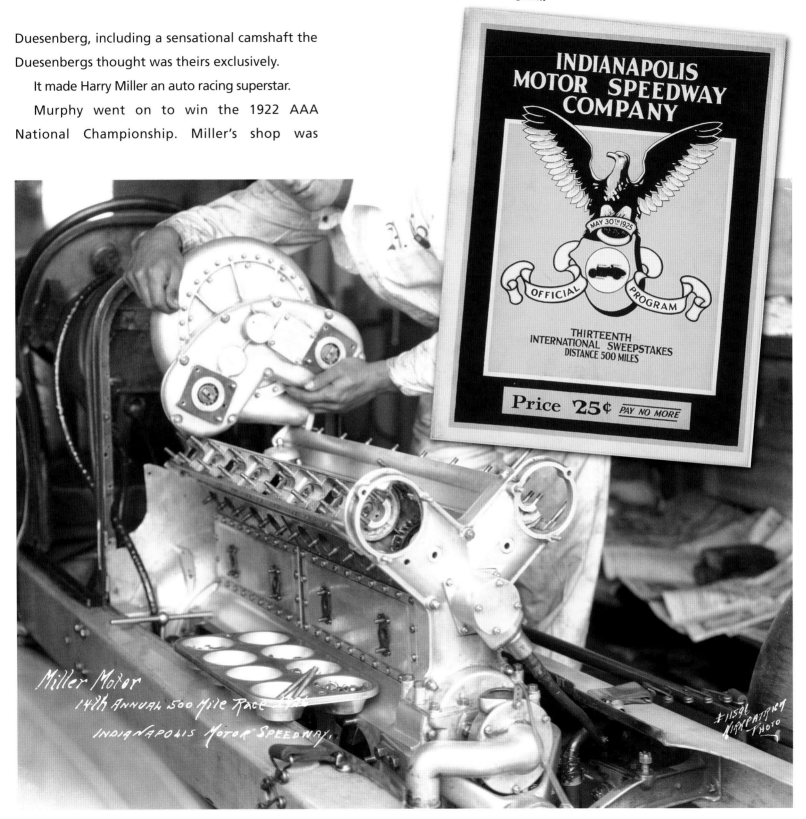

Here's what a partly assembled mid-'20s Miller engine looked like. That's the centrifugal supercharger added to the back.

1926 program.

suddenly awash in engine orders. Soon, he was building whole cars. For much of the next half-century, machinery carrying Miller DNA dominated Indianapolis.

Books have been written about Miller, the dapper little man from Wisconsin with an unfathomable mind and an artist's touch. He was shy, candid to a fault, and disturbingly clairvoyant. His worried wife, Edna, believed he knew what she was saying before she said it. He had an uncanny habit of correctly predicting when people would die. His Malibu Canyon ranch was a veritable zoo, swarming with all manner of birds and animals. He kept a parrot in his drafting room and a monkey on the seat beside him when he went for a drive.

Miller had opened his machine shop in Los Angeles about the time Carl Fisher was getting serious about building his speedway. Before long, young Fred Offenhauser was working for him.

George Hunt poses with the 1929 Studebaker President pace car.

Track announcers in their perch atop the pagoda in 1929.

When master draftsman Leo Goosen came aboard in 1919, the brain trust was in place. Miller was the idea man. He had them in glorious profusion. Leo did the drawings. Fred fashioned the parts.

But Miller, himself, would eventually become a victim of his great success.

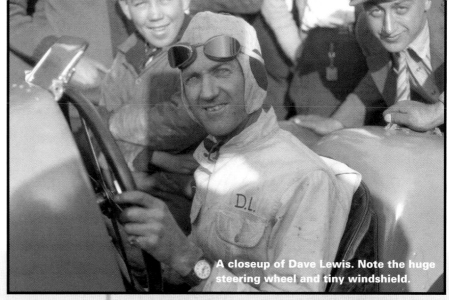

A closeup of Dave Lewis. Note the huge steering wheel and tiny windshield.

Here's Harry Miller's handiwork at its finest. With Dave Lewis driving, the first front-wheel-drive Miller at Indianapolis finished second in 1925. The front-wheel-drive layout was easy on tires, lowered the center of gravity, and made cornering a little quicker.

Lester Maitland
strikes a
pose with the
checkered flag
in 1928.

This view of the cockpit of Ralph Hepburn's Miller in 1929 gives perspective to the huge steering wheel and to Hepburn's obstructed sightline.

Coveted VIP parking behind the pits was a pricey perk for half a century. Check out the attire in this 1928 photo.

Following purchase of the Speedway in 1927 by Eddie Rickenbacker and some wealthy Detroiters, a radical rules package was drawn up effectively outlawing Miller's high-priced hardware and luring the "little guy" and mainstream carmakers back to the "500." It went into effect with the 1930 race.

By 1934, Harry Miller was bankrupt.

A sea of people crowd around the "bull pen" area where victory celebrations occurred in the early days.

Crowd Indianapolis Motor Speedway 1926.

#11646 KIRKPATRICK PHOTO

RACING ON A SHOESTRING
1930-1939

I think what the spectator wants to see is the crash, the action, the car splitting apart. The more flame the better. The more wheels that zip off into orbit the better. But the fan wants the driver to jump out alive and wave to the crowd because that's the moment of greatest thrill. That's when man has conquered his machine, and therefore, the spectator's dream of immortality is confirmed.

— *Racer/commentator Sam Posey*

Check out the log chain holding Louis Meyer's No. 8 Ring-Free Miller in place on this makeshift dynamometer in 1936. Meyer's dominance of the latter stages of the race brought him his third "500" victory.

It's conventional wisdom that the Great Depression had a negative impact on the Indianapolis 500. After all, it did on everything else.

But maybe not.

From year to year during the '30s the size of Memorial Day throngs at the Speedway crept upwards. And contrary to expectations, draconian rule changes that lowered costs and gave the

Louis Meyer

Three-time "500" winner Louis Meyer saw action at the race for the first time in 1927, when he drove relief for the great Wilbur Shaw. He won in '28, '33, and '36. He and Dale Drake bought Fred Offenhauser's engine business in '46 and nurtured the venerable Offy through another 20 years of front-running Indy action.

"500" a whole new face actually produced faster qualifying and race speeds. The ancient axiom about necessity being the mother of invention was proven again and again.

True, '30s "500" racers dipped into a smaller pot of gold, but considering the terrible financial straits confronting most Americans, the $18,000 Louis Meyer's team took home for winning the '33 race was still eye-popping. That was, by far, the worst Indianapolis 500 payday of the decade. For winning the '34 race, Bill Cummings got $29,000.

Carl Fisher's trickle-down formula was still working. Make the event unique enough and the payoff big enough to lure hot cars and the hottest shoes. Make rules to assure a show unlike anything spectators will find anywhere else. Then, open the gates and stand back.

Some fine-tuning soon took a little of the sting out of it, but the 1930 rules package turned the old guard on its ear. With the stroke of a pen, the

Taking a break from the racing wars, Louis Meyer and Peter DePaolo get in some golf on the new course Eddie Rickenbacker had built at the Speedway.

Jimmie Booth and Larry Wall, wearing the famed flying wing coveralls that identify them as Duesenberg team members, assemble an engine in 1931.

The 1930 Cord L-29 pace car, piloted by Wade Morton.

Two race cars have been dismantled and are in the process of re-assembly in Louis Meyer's Indianapolis shop in 1931.

"TROPHIES AND PRIZES"

The Borg-Warner Trophy may be the most famous, but arguably the most grandiose of Indianapolis trophies has to be the ancient eight-foot tall, sterling silver Wheeler-Schebler. Presented as a traveling trophy for the main-event races of 1909-10, it was then retired. Reappearing in 1913, it was awarded for the next 20 years to whichever car was leading at the 400-mile mark. A 1909 deed declared the trophy the permanent property of the first owner whose cars won it three times, provided they were the same make. Harry Hartz (second from the right below) met the criteria in 1932. The trophy has been displayed in the Hall of Fame Museum since the mid-'50s. Another big prize since 1936 has been the pace car (or a replica). That's Tony Hulman waving from the driver's seat of the Corvette that paced the '78 race (bottom).

Borg-Warner Trophy.

1978 pace car.

Wheeler-Schebler Trophy flanked by Jerry Houck and Fred Frame on the left and Harry Hartz and Jean Marcenac on the right.

AAA contest board sidelined the thoroughbred Duesenbergs and Millers with their supercharged engines and $15,000 price tags.

Two-man cars like those that last raced at Indy in 1922 were back. They had to weigh at least 1,750 pounds, up from 1,400. Supercharging was out, as were overhead camshafts with multi-valve cylinder heads and exotic multi-barrel carburetors. So-called stock-block engines could displace up to six liters. They would have less power, but they cost less, too.

The goal was to return racing to the less well-heeled, of which, it was hoped, there would be quite a few. It was a wise idea. Only 36 entries had been filed for the 1928 "500." There were 70 in 1931.

It was also hoped that altering the playing field would entice America's passenger car companies

Until several sets of lights (one yellow, one green) were installed around the track in 1935, workers used yellow flags to warn drivers of perilous conditions.

Bill Cummings

Local boy and crowd favorite Bill Cummings, whose dad was a race driver before him, grew up four miles from the Speedway. Listening from home, it is said he could identify some of the cars by the sound of their engines. He drove taxi cabs and ran a tavern, but a promise to his mother as a youngster that he would one day win the "500" was fulfilled with a popular victory in 1934. His average speed was a tick below 105 mph, a track record.

Cliff Bergere

Cliff Bergere's first "500" was in 1927. He started from the pole in '46. He appeared in dozens of movies, where he was an extra or a stunt double. But he might be best remembered for what precipitated his retirement in 1950. Assigned to one of Lew Welch's infamous Novi machines, he spun twice in practice. When he mentioned he thought the car unsafe, Welch unceremoniously replaced him with another popular Indy veteran, Ralph Hepburn. On the Sunday of pole qualifying weekend, Hepburn lost control of the car and perished in the subsequent crash.

CLIFF BERGERE, 1935.

back into the game. A few gave it a shot. Studebaker was there in '32 and '33 with a highly-regarded five-car factory effort. Running gear was near stock. Engines were straight-eights hot-rodded by factory engineers to about 200 horsepower. Cliff Bergere drove one to a third-place finish in '32.

But the most notable factory program was the 1935 Ford invasion. At the urging of super-salesman Preston Tucker, young Edsel Ford hired Harry Miller to craft 10 beautiful front-drive cars. A least nine were built. Powered by modified stock-block Ford engines, four made the race. This $200,000 project (in 1934 dollars) went for naught when the Fords all succumbed to steering gear failure as engine heat boiled away the lubricant.

It would be three decades before Indianapolis would see another Ford factory program. That one would be immensely more successful.

While maestro Harry Miller (center) and driver Ted Horn stand by, a AAA official measures how much fuel Horn has used on his qualifying run for the '35 race. He started 26th, finished 16th.

The battery pack needed to service the Cummins Diesel in 1931 weighed approximately 100 pounds. It got hauled around in this toy wagon.

MILLER SIXTEEN

Rule changes produced a marvelous array of engines in the early '30s. Here's a 1932 Miller V16 made from two straight-eights on a common crankcase. It was fast but not very durable.

THE STUDEBAKER FLEET

INDIANAPOLIS MOTOR SPEEDWAY - 1932.

Bringing passenger carmakers back to Indianapolis was a main objective of Eddie Rickenbacker's radical rules package. Five Studebakers made the race in 1932.

1930 program.

As ugly as it was, however, the Ford fiasco wasn't the worst thing about the 1935 race. Wrecks during practice and qualifications took the lives of two drivers and a riding mechanic. There was another fatality and more injuries in the race.

Bad crashes, too many of them fatal, had marred every "500" since the 1930 rules went into effect. The cars, many of them made out of inexpensive passenger vehicle parts, were heavier and faster. In the hands of hard-nosed drivers, they were turning the "500" into a demolition derby. Now 20 years old, the track needed a major a rehab, which would occur after the '35 race.

But what to do in the meantime?

Oil had been a problem from Day One at Indianapolis, when exposed valve gear and primitive gravity-flow lube systems meant hundreds of gallons bled onto the track in the course of a race. As puddles formed, workmen went out amid the traffic and shoveled sand on them. The resultant slurry was said to make the bricks even slicker.

Stubby Stubblefield was at the wheel of this swoopy Miller-powered creation in 1932. He started 26th, finished 14th.

The official pace car of the 1933 race, the Chrysler Imperial driven by Byron Foy.

By the mid-30s, the "500" field was rife with production-based machinery. Remove and reshape enough body panels and a Hudson passenger car could be turned into something like the Miller car Deacon Litz drove in 1935.

Hartwell "Stubby" Stubblefield was on his 10-lap qualifying run for the 1935 race when a steering arm failure sent his car over the wall. He and riding mechanic Leo Whittaker both perished. Here's what's left of his car.

The Bowes Seal Fast garage was a busy place before the '35 race. That's a four-cylinder Miller engine on the workbench.

Rex Mays

Hard-luck Rex Mays, one of Indy's most popular drivers, was a sprint car star in California before his Speedway debut in 1934. In 12 Indianapolis 500 starts, he was on the pole four times. Twice, he finished second. Hired in '49 to drive the Novi that had been rebuilt after the '48 Hepburn crash, he started second behind fellow Novi pilot Duke Nalon. Avoiding the flames from Nalon's awful crash on Lap 24, he led the race until his engine failed on Lap 48.

To make the track less like a skating rink, the AAA Contest Board imposed a six-gallon per car oil consumption limit in '33. But that wasn't all. It reduced the size of fuel tanks from 45 to 15 gallons, thus assuring more pit stops and the opportunity for more tire and wheel inspections.

Still, bad crashes led to the deaths of five drivers and riding mechanics during practice and the '33 race itself.

While the newspapers argued whether it was the thrill of the race or pure bloodlust that kept the crowds coming back, officials opted in 1934 to hold the field to 33 cars and to reduce speeds by limiting total fuel consumption to 45 gallons. Going the distance meant de-tuning the car. "Unproven" drivers could also voluntarily submit to a sort of driver's test, where scrutineers reviewed their actions on the track. In a couple of years, it would become mandatory.

Renowned chief mechanic Phil Shafer examines a piston out of a Miller straight-eight.

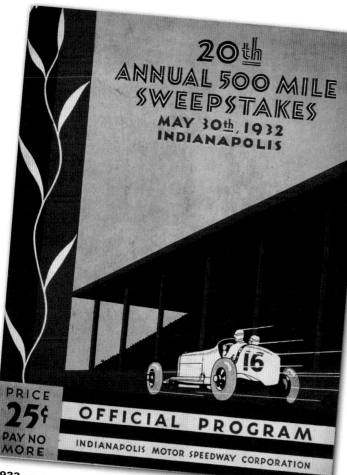

1932 program.

Although two died in a crash during practice, the 1934 race was fatality-free. By adjusting compression and carburetion, and by gearing for slower engine rpms, Bill Cummings won it at a record average of just under 105 miles an hour.

That wasn't the slow-down the rule-makers hoped for. So, they pulled out more stops in 1935. Helmets were now required for drivers and riding mechanics. Yellow caution lights were installed in six spots around the track. And to force more de-tuning, the fuel allotment was lowered still more—to 42.5 gallons.

But nothing seemed to work.

A hot-shot East coast dirt track racer named

That's a police car leading the way through the main gate into the track in 1930. Notice the Prest-O-Lite smokestack in the background. It was a Speedway landmark for more than half a century.

Big Boy Rader led the way in the 1934 race with this LaSalle pace car.

"TRADITIONS OF THE INDY 500"

For the better part of 40 years, Larry Bisceglia's van was first in line for the "500."

Jim Nabors first sang "Back Home Again in Indiana" in 1972 and has entertained spectators nearly every year since. Here, he sings in 2006.

Movie star Arlene Dahl gives Troy Ruttman a victory kiss in 1952.

The milk, the wreath, the Borg-Warner Trophy and Rick Mears in 1991.

Mari Hulman George continues the "start your engines" ritual that began in the late '40s.

From 1947 through 1954, "Water from Wilbur" was what "500" winners drank in Victory Lane.

The Art Koch family from Pittsburgh has had seats at the "500" since 1960.

Indianapolis 500 race time is party time for thousands.

Johnny Hannon, who was new to the "500," didn't take the voluntary driver's test. He became a fatality when he crashed in the third turn of his first practice lap. Later that day, Indy veteran Hartwell "Stubby" Stubblefield and his mechanic both perished when their car went over the outside wall in Turn 1. And it wasn't over yet. They repaired Hannon's car, which was then qualified by young Clay Weatherly. He died when he crashed coming out of Turn 4 early in the race.

Colorful Kelly Petillo ended up the winner.

Karl Kizer, a Tony Hulman confidant who would spearhead the post-war creation of the Speedway's Hall of Fame Museum, was the proprietor of a machine shop during the Depression where many local racers sent their repair work. That's where he was when Petillo walked in a couple of days before the race.

1933 program.

PRICE 25¢ PAY NO MORE

TWENTY - FIRST INTERNATIONAL 500 MILE SWEEPSTAKES

OFFICIAL PROGRAM

MAY 30TH 1933

INDIANAPOLIS MOTOR SPEEDWAY CORPORATION

At the height of the Great Depression, Eddie Rickenbacker dug deep for the resources to rehab the corners, rebuild outside walls, and rip out interior walls that had aggravated safety conditions at the Speedway for a number of years.

"His engine had blown up. He begged me to fix it," Kizer remembered years later. "We were completely swamped. I told him I couldn't do it. He came back about 5:15 that afternoon with his wife and kid. He started to cry. He said he had every dime invested in the car and that he only had $18.26 to live on between now and the race.

"I didn't want the job, but I looked over at Petillo's little kid and it didn't seem fair for him to go hungry. So I told Kelly we would help him out. We made new pistons and rods and some other stuff and we welded up his block. The work came to around $800. We called the car The Welded Wonder.

"Well, by golly if Kelly didn't go out there and win the race. And the next morning he ran all the way from the bank to our shop to pay off his debt."

Petillo's share of the $78,575 purse was $30,600.

1930 ticket.

1933 ticket.

Notice the new dirt apron on the inside of the turn. Of the many improvements made before the 1936 race, racers said they most appreciated those new run-off areas.

SHAW AT FINISH OF RACE

H4920
KIRKPATRICK
INDIANAPOLIS.

Wilbur Shaw had notched his first Indy 500 victory in 1937, and he's telling the world about it via radio. WIRE was a popular Indianapolis station.

Drivers and riding mechanics could still wear whatever headgear they liked in the early '30s. Wilbur Shaw has opted for one of the first hard helmets in '32. His riding mechanic went with more conventional leather.

Even motorcycle fans liked to watch the "500."

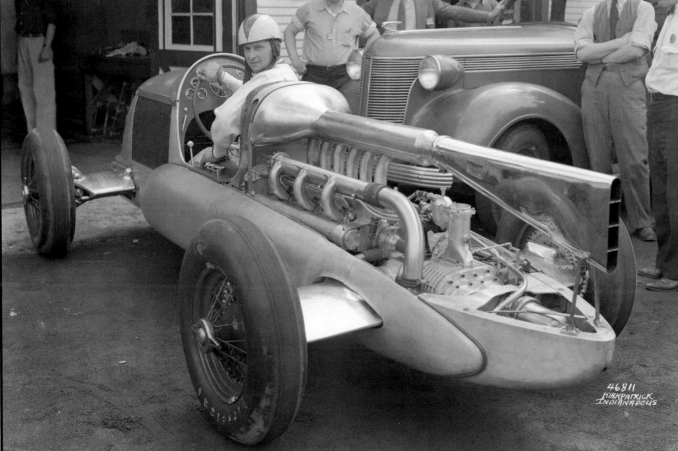

Harry Miller intended to have two revolutionary rear engine cars ready for the '38 race. He got one running. Ralph Hepburn was behind the wheel for a few practice laps, but time ran out before he could attempt to qualify.

The dirt began to fly at the Speedway the day after the '35 race. Before they were done, work crews had ripped out inside retaining walls and curbs and created nice big aprons on the inside of each curve. They rebuilt and re-paved all four corners, eliminating a steeper-angled lip at the very top that had become a sort of launching ramp.

They also reconfigured the outside retaining walls so they were perpendicular to the banking, not the horizon. Whether it was the rehab or another mandated reduction in the fuel allotment or just plain luck, the '36 race was fatality-free.

It also established new traditions on several fronts. The milk-drinking tradition that still endures was started when Louis Meyer drank a bottle of buttermilk in Victory Lane. This was also the first year for the Borg-Warner Trophy and for the addition of the pace car (or a reasonable facsimile) to the winner's haul.

Satisfied that his rehab money was well spent, Eddie Rickenbacker ordered more upgrades,

Dressed in his Sunday best and with his ever-present pipe at hand, Mauri Rose looks nothing like the grimy short-tempered guy Indianapolis 500 race fans of the '30s and '40s had come to know. This is 1938. Notice the barbed wire separating the pits from the spectators.

While they're waiting in pre-dawn darkness for the track to open, these young men have turned their car into a cozy card room.

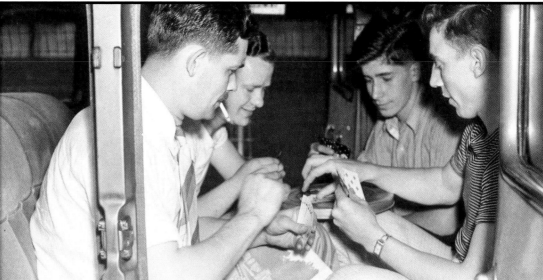

1935 ticket.

Just as it has been for 100 years, the "500" was an excuse in the late '30s to party down. Since Prohibition was repealed in 1933, it's a good bet that's not ginger ale in those bottles.

A pre-war Maserati engine is being put together by Henry "Cotton" Henning, Wibur Shaw's chief mechanic in the late '30s. Fully assembled, there would be another cylinder head above the crankcase.

including asphalt paving over the backstretch. By 1940, the original bricks were buried everywhere except the front straight.

Rickenbaker and "Pop" Myers were also able to persuade a recalcitrant Indianapolis 500 racing establishment to open the door again to European Grand Prix machinery. The resultant two-stage adjustment of the rules in '37 and '38 spelled the end of the two-man car, brought the supercharger back, and triggered another wonderful rush of technical innovation.

Wilbur Shaw's penchant for vaulting guard rails found him flipping this Duesenberg at Ascot in California later in 1931.

That's Wilbur Shaw's No. 32 Duesenburg hurtling over the wall in this retouched 1931 photo. Out of the Speedway hospital about an hour later, Shaw took over the No. 33 Duesenberg and rejoined the race. Drivers who witnessed Shaw's wreck and then saw him back in action thought they were seeing a ghost.

Here's a typical late '30s garage scene.

A stout hauler was required to transport the thousands of pounds of bricks that were dug up and reset in the mid and late-'30s.

Louis Schwitzer, winner of the first race (a 5-miler in 1909) held at the Speedway, became a highly regarded AAA official. The Schwitzer Award for engineering excellence, presented each May, is named after him.

The flying wheel, a Speedway logo from the beginning, floats over the main gate in 1947.

SURVIVING THE WAR YEARS
1940-1949

The Speedway has always been a part of Indiana, as the derby is part of Kentucky. The 500-Mile Race should be continued. I'd just like to be sure of sufficient income so we could make a few improvements each year...

— Tony Hulman, 1945

To me the track was the last great speed shrine, which must be preserved at all cost. I felt that all I was, or ever hoped to be, I owed to the Indianapolis 500-Mile Race.

— Wilbur Shaw, 1954

Since 1936, "500" winners have been awarded the pace car. Or a reasonable facsimile, anyway. Presentation ceremonies have ranged from a simple handover of the keys to major news conferences. In 1940, Speedway General Manager "Pop" Myers and "500" champ Wilbur Shaw stood for this photo op.

As the 1940s loomed at the Indianapolis 500, the guttural bark of four-cylinder Offenhausers was joined by the scream of supercharged sixes and eights. The Offys had company.

That was what Speedway owner Eddie Rickenbacker had in mind when he orchestrated the adoption of the International Grand Prix

Wilbur Shaw

Wilbur Shaw won the "500" three times and was headed toward a fourth in '41 when a wheel failed. But even more than his racing exploits, Shaw will be remembered for his role in resurrecting the Speedway after World War II. He brought Eddie Rickenbacker and Tony Hulman together in November 1945. Shaw was the public face of the Indianapolis 500 as Speedway president until his death in a plane crash in 1954.

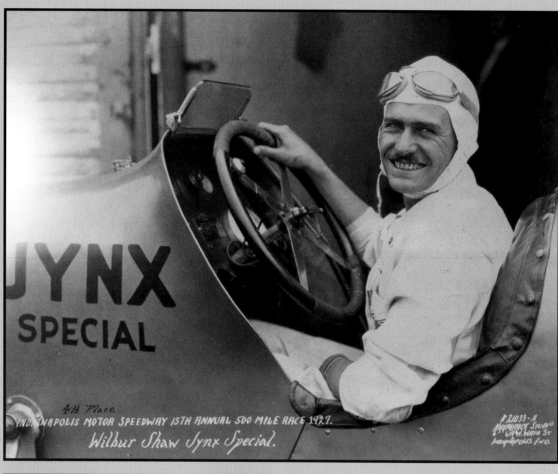

engine formula. He was betting it would add an exotic extra dimension to his Indy 500 spectacle. It did.

Not surprisingly, master draftsman Leo Goosen, whose handiwork included the Millers of the '20s and the Offys of the '30s, was in on the design of some of the new machinery. He drew the new Art Sparks straight six and both a straight eight and a V8 for the Winfield brothers. When the thundering Novi that would mesmerize race fans for years to come first appeared in 1946, it was was fitted with the Winfield V8.

With the welcome mat out to European machinery, an Alfa Romeo was the first through

Not much was left of George Barringer's rear-engine slant-six supercharged Miller after an explosion and fire destroyed several garages race day morning in 1941.

A pre-war ritual in the run-up to the "500": Men with brooms sweeping the track.

"PAGODAS THROUGH THE CENTURY"

Maybe it is the incongruity, but for much of the last 100 years, structures vaguely reminiscent of an ancient Buddhist temple have been as symbolic of the Indianapolis 500 as the bricks long buried beneath the asphalt track. Carl Fisher had the first one built at the starting line to house race control in 1913. Somebody labeled it a pagoda, and the name stuck. A second more grandiose structure replaced it in 1926 and was, itself, replaced by a stark glass and steel control tower in 1957. The newest pagoda replaced the tower in 2000. It has nine viewing levels and reaches a height equal to a 13-story building, not including the 46-foot flagpole at the top. Glass panels facing the main straightaway were specially built in England.

1913 to 1925.

1926 to 1956.

1957 to 1999.

2000 to present.

the door. Rex Mays qualified an Alfa on the front row in '38.

But it was left to Wilbur Shaw, a native of nearby Shelbyville, Indiana, to put a foreign car in Victory Lane for the first time in 20 years. It was 1939. The car was a beautiful deep purple Maserati owned by "Umbrella" Mike Boyle, the flamboyant Chicago labor leader, and prepared by Henry "Cotton" Henning, one of Indy's all-time great mechanics. Shaw won again in 1940 with the same car. Nobody had ever done that before.

Students of Indianapolis 500 racing agree the Maserati was a splendid piece of work. A lowered frame featured boxed-section side rails that were tied together in the rear by a massive magnesium casting, which doubled as the oil tank. Whereas American cars had rudimentary mechanical brakes that were used mostly for pit stops, the Maserati had hydraulic 16-inch magnesium drums front and rear.

Shaw exercised them with gusto.

Great brakes let him drive deep into the corners while everybody else was coasting. The engine wasn't that powerful, but twin gear-driven Roots-type superchargers delivered the mid-range torque that permitted Shaw to accelerate out of the corners faster than anybody.

The popular three-time Indy champ would drive his last "500" in 1941. He was leading with 48 laps to go when a wheel broke, sending his handsome Maserati backward into the wall. The impact split his fuel tank, drenching him with gasoline. If that weren't bad enough, a brace came loose and, like a battering ram, clobbered

INDY PROFILE

Clarence Cagle

As a youngster, Clarence Cagle remembered spending about as much time with the Hulman family as he did his own. Appointed grounds superintendent in 1947, he took enormous pride in the property's appearance and condition. Until his retirement almost 30 years later, Cagle kept the Speedway true to Hulman's vision.

Mauri Rose

Mauri Rose was a no-nonsense GM engineer assigned to the Allison Division after WW II. He would drive from the plant to the track during lunch hour, dazzle everybody with a few fast laps, then go back to work. His come-from-far-behind victory in 1941 in a car teammate Floyd Davis had started brought him notoriety. His consecutive wins in 1947 and '48 made him famous. Among several high-level positions he held after he quit driving in '51 was one as chief development engineer on Chevrolet's new Corvette.

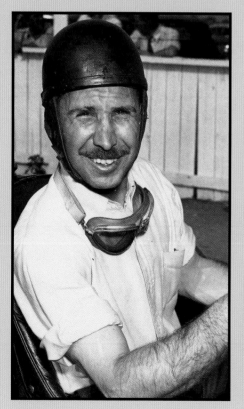

Shaw in the lower spine. Partially paralyzed, Shaw coolly directed his rescuers not to move him until his back was stabilized.

Rickenbacker was in New York December 7, 1941, and just as Carl Fisher had done in 1917, one of the first things he did after Pearl Harbor was to offer the use of the Speedway to the War Department. To his great surprise, it was refused.

Rickenbacker quickly directed Pop Myers to close the office near downtown Indianapolis. The track's big wooden entrance gates at the corner of 16th Street and Georgetown Road were padlocked. And Rickenbacker's brother Al was installed to watch over the place. He moved a desk into a little building that also served as the starter house for

Three-time Grand Prix champion Rudolf Caracciola, whose European racing exploits made him a legend, was supposed to drive a Mercedes in the '46 race. But when it was held up in customs, an injured Joel Thorne offered him this car. That's Thorne in the wheelchair. After Caracciola was seriously injured in a crash during practice, he convalesced in Tony Hulman's Terre Haute, Indiana, lodge. Years later, his family transferred the dozens of trophies and trappings of his long career to the Hall of Fame Museum, where they are on display.

1941 Chrysler Newport pace car driven by A.B. Couture.

Russ Snowberger's Maserati and Hal Robson's Miller-powered Bugatti are alongside each other as they negotiate the front straight in 1946.

1946 program.

Give Mother Nature her way and here's what she did to the Speedway during World War II.

the golf course Rickenbacker had built soon after buying the place in 1927.

And that's the way it stayed through four winters. About the only human activity at the Speedway involved neighborhood kids swimming in the tunnels after heavy rains, or hunting rabbits in the winter and mushrooms in the spring. Weeds, shrubs and wildflowers took root in the cracks between the front stretch bricks. The spiffy white paint with green accents that covered the multitude of buildings and miles of board fences faded and chipped. Bleacher seats rotted. Trees sprouted. The fire-damaged garage area became a tangled thicket.

That's how Wilbur Shaw found the place around Thanksgiving, 1944, when his team of Firestone people showed up to run a tire test. The firm had developed a synthetic rubber tire; the mission was to mount a set on a race car and run it 500 miles at speeds sufficiently high to satisfy the government that they would the hold up in general use.

While he was clearing a path and running the test, Shaw viewed the desolation and vowed not to let the place die.

"To me the track was the world's last great speed shrine, which must be preserved at any cost," he said. "I felt that all I was, or ever hoped to be, I owed to the Indianapolis 500 Mile Race."

Shaw's next moves were a lot like Carl Fisher's in 1909, when the awful sight of thousands of empty seats unleashed the creative juices that produced the once-a-year spectacle of the "500."

Now a man on a mission, he went to see Rickenbacker, who allowed that, yes, indeed, the track was for sale. He talked to bankers and

Automobiles disappear into a sea of people on the Georgetown Road side of the Speedway in 1948.

1940 ticket.

Ignited fuel from Duke Nalon's fiery crash in 1949 has washed across the track, forcing eventual winner Bill Holland almost into the grass.

1947 program.

That's driver Spider Webb in the Grancor entry. He started 26th in 1949, but suffered transmission failure on race morning and could not start.

industrialists, and finally, to Anton "Tony" Hulman, the wholesale grocery magnate from Terre Haute, Indiana. Wilbur especially liked the fact that Tony had no stake in the automobile business.

An off-the-cuff Hulman comment during their meeting has served as a kind of mission statement at the track ever since: "The Speedway has always been a part of Indiana, as the Derby is part of Kentucky. The 500-Mile race should be continued. I'd just like to be sure of sufficient income so we could make a few improvements each year, and make the track something everybody can be proud of."

On November 14, 1945, Rickenbacker signed the deed over to Hulman, who paid him $750,000, almost exactly what "Rick" bought the track for 18 years earlier. In another brilliant move that indicated the Hulman team could negotiate with the best, an agreement was soon made with the famous Jacobs brothers of Buffalo to handle concessions at the track. It's been said that deal covered the purchase price with several thousand dollars left over to finance the rehab.

Hulman vowed there would be a race on Memorial Day, 1946. And a race there was.

Shaw, who had been named president, became the public face of the Speedway. Pop Myers and Dolly re-opened the Speedway office near downtown Indianapolis, and started selling tickets. Superintendent Jack Fortner soon had several hundred laborers on the grounds from daylight till dark undoing the havoc Mother Nature had wreaked upon the Speedway.

The track was in good enough shape to open for practice May 1. When the public gates were opened on the 15th, spectators mixed with workmen who were still painting and patching and pouring concrete.

Race day was bedlam. Stuck in long, slow-moving lines, cars overheated by the hundreds. It might have been routine in pre-war days to exaggerate the size of the crowd, but nobody quarreled with an estimate of 100,000 for the 1946 race.

Somehow, Shaw had unearthed enough machinery to fill the 33-car field. Almost everything was pre-war vintage. But Paul Russo qualified on the front row in the Fageol Twin Coach Spl., a new contraption featuring two Offy midget engines, one in front, the other behind the driver, and four-wheel-drive, which was accomplished by the use of two front-drive units Fageol had rescued from the 1935 Miller Ford debacle. It crashed on Lap 16.

The crowd favorite, however, was car No. 2, a long, low screamer driven by popular 50-year-old Ralph Hepburn. His 133.9 mph qualifying speed had obliterated the track record. The first in Lew Welch's string of magnificent Novi machines, they would deliver stardom, pain, and heartache to some of America's greatest drivers over the next 20 years. But they wouldn't win a "500."

Hepburn started 19th. By Lap 12 he was the leader. Running nine to 10 miles an hour faster than anybody else, he was ahead by more than a minute when a long pit stop dropped him to 13th. To the enormous disappointment of the assembled throng, a dropped valve put him out of the race on Lap 122. Many spectators immediately headed for the exits, which were blocked by people still trying to get in.

1947 ticket.

British-born George Robson won the race. His share of the first "500" purse to exceed $100,000 was $42,550.

Feisty Wilbur Shaw found himself in a dispute with his many driver friends in 1947, when some of them, as members of ASPAR, the American Society of Professional Auto Racing, threatened to boycott the "500." They thought the purse ought to be several times bigger. With local sports editor Bill Fox the go-between, the track and the group finally came to terms.

Of the 30 cars lined up for the start, two were Lou Moore's brand-new front-drive Blue Crown Spark Plug specials. Mauri Rose and Bill Holland were his drivers. Rose would take this win, and the next one, too. Holland would win in 1949.

1946 press ticket.

"CELEBRATIONS AND CEREMONIES"

In the 100-plus years since cornfields and pastureland were turned into a playground unlike any in all the world, tens of millions have entered the gates of the Indianapolis Motor Speedway to witness a 500-mile race. Millions more have tuned in via radio and television. They departed, each and every one, indelibly imprinted.

Bill Vukovich's 1952 debut of the first "roadster" signaled the beginning of the end for open cockpit cars such as these, with drivers straddling the driveshaft and their upper bodies clearly visible from the grandstands.

ROADSTERS REIGN SUPREME
1950-1959

Whether or not the threatened driver strike in 1947 had anything to do with it, the pot of gold that lured the gladiators to the Indianapolis 500 every year surged to $215,000 by 1950.

As Fisher had long before predicted, the purse was both a perennial sore point and an irresistible lure. Indy "500" participants who thought it too

Tony Hulman

For a while after Speedway President Wilbur Shaw's death in late 1954, people wondered who Tony Hulman would hire to replace him. Tony ended speculation in typical Hulman style by allowing as how he might just tackle the job himself. He did so with flair and grace until his own death in late 1977.

small came close to unionizing in 1947. In 1949, Lewis Welch's insistence on appearance money cost his two Novi cars a chance to make the race. But as the '50s dawned, the prospect of an ever richer payday had Indy's master innovators working wonders with their racing machinery.

Just as the Peugeots were so carefully dissected and duplicated in the early days, the best ideas didn't stay secret very long. Take the Blue Crown Spark Plug cars. Lou Moore had worried with the design for years before his drivers, Mauri Rose and Bill Holland, blew the "500" away with back-to-back one-two finishes in 1947 and '48 and, for good measure, another win in '49. By then, several copies were already on the "500" grid. Fred Offenhauser had sold his engine business to Louis Meyer and Dale Drake in 1946, and over the next five years they brought the Offy into the modern age. They experimented with forged pistons and more radical camshaft profiles. They switched from old-school poured babbitt engine bearings, which needed to be renewed every four or five races, to the kind already in wide use in production autos. Racers discovered the bearing would last an entire season on the so-called Champ car circuit.

Since virtually every Champ car already had an Offy in its engine bay, and since cost containment was a big issue, the primary Meyer/Drake objective was increased durability, not necessarily power.

Stu Hilborn soon came along. The California hot-rodder had devised a bolt-on fuel-injection unit for smaller Offy-powered midget racers. It went over so well that taking a crack at the little Offy's 300-horse big brother seemed the logical thing to do.

Stu did it and dynamometer results were impressive. He had found an instant 10 percent boost in horsepower. Set up for qualifying in '49, fuel injection was thought to deliver a three-to-five mile-per-hour speed advantage at the "500." Word spread, and Hilborn had a new profit center.

In that era, you could qualify on fuel injection and switch to carburetors for the race. Since a fuel-

Movie star Clark Gable shakes hands with driver Pat Flaherty in 1950. Some scenes of Gable's racing movie *To Please a Lady* **were filmed at the track.**

The extensive sponsor involvement at the Indianapolis 500 through the years is fitting of the world's most famous race.

"SPONSORS AND ADVERTISING"

LER CARBURETORS

MICHELIN TIRES

RAYFIELD CARBURETOR

Accessory suppliers were part of the Speedway scene from the get-go.

SPEED KINGS LIKE FLORSHEI

WILBUR SHAW 2nd Place = LOUIS MEYER

Billy Devore had candy company backing in 1941.

Superstars Wilbur Shaw, Louis Meyer and Lou Moore get outfitted with Florsheim shoes in 1933.

The "Indiana Jones" theme of Marco Andretti's 2008 Indy sponsorship extended to his trackside apparel.

In addition to its title sponsorship of the IndyCar Series, IZOD backed Ryan Hunter-Reay's No. 37 in the 2010 race.

Fuel tanks double as sponsor billboards.

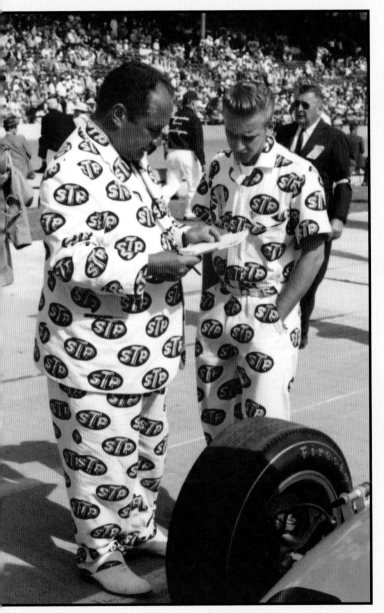

STP maestro Andy Granatelli had his suit tailor-made for the '67 race.

injected engine got less mileage than a carbureted Offy, it didn't see much race action until higher speeds, and the resultant tire wear, meant nobody could go the distance on less than three or four pit stops. By 1953, tire wear dictated pit stop intervals, and almost every Offy on the grid was equipped with one of Hilborn's fuel injection units.

With the exception of two Cummins Diesels, the occasional Novi V8, a single Ferrari, and a rogue stock-block Buick or Chevy, entire 33-car fields at Indianapolis from 1951 through the early '60s and then again in the '70s, were Offy-powered.

It's interesting that the Offy and the roadster are merged in much of the public mind, but the Offy was around for more than 40 years while the roadster only ruled for 15.

Pole sitter Pat Flaherty, who would win in the first roadster built by A.J. Watson, brings the field to a near perfect start in 1956. That's Jim Rathmann in the middle of the front row and Pat O'Connor on the outside.

Popular Fred Agabashian's Cummins turbo/diesel—not the first diesel at Indy but the first turbo by a decade—was one of two radical cars Frank Kurtis built for the 1952 race. Kurtis virtually owned the booming midget racer market in California but was relatively unknown in Indy car circles. That would soon change.

The Diesel was a ponderous beast. At about 2,500 pounds, it weighed half again as much as the typical early 1950s "500" car. Its 6.8-liter engine cranked out almost 400 horsepower. Fred put it on the pole, but eventually quit the race with a clogged turbo inlet.

The other car was smaller, but under the skin it had some of the same architecture. Both cars had the driver seated low and far to the right. Both had engines offset to the left and tilted so the driveshaft ran alongside the driver, not under him. The setup not only reduced frontal area and lowered the center of gravity, it produced a left-side weight bias that greatly improved tire grip in the corners.

The smaller of the two cars, Bill Vukovich's grey and yellow No. 26 Fuel Injection, is universally hailed as Indy's first "roadster." Vuky dominated the 1952 race until a steering arm failed 22 laps short of the finish.

With Vuky's fine ride, the die was cast. The quest for the perfect combination of low center of gravity and optimum left-side weight bias would take many forms in the years ahead. But with the appearance of No. 26, the roadster era was born.

Vuky went on to win the "500" in 1953 (with the lap prize fund now at $150 per lap, his share of the purse was almost $90,000). He won again in '54, and by 1955, Kurtis-Kraft roadsters made up more than half of the "500" starting field.

The exciting roadster story notwithstanding, 1955 was a bad year for the Speedway. It started

A.J. Watson

A.J. Watson was chief mechanic on Bob Sweikert's 1955 "500" winner, but his rise to the front rank of race car builders really started in 1956, when the radical roadster he crafted for Pat Flaherty started on the pole and ended up in Victory Lane. Watson roadsters also won the "500" in 1959, '60, '62 '63 and '64.

Finally giving up on front-drive, Lewis Welch installed his powerful Novi engines into a pair of rear-drive cars for 1956. This is one of them. Paul Russo was leading when a blown tire led to a crash on Lap 22.

1950 program.

OFFICIAL PROGRAM
34th 500 MILE RACE
MAY 30, 1950

50¢ PAY NO MORE

INDIANAPOLIS MOTOR SPEEDWAY CORPORATION

October 30, 1954, when Wilbur Shaw and two others died in a small plane crash near Decatur, Indiana. That left the Speedway without a president.

In the months ahead, racing accidents in the U.S. and abroad would nearly kill the sport. The American Automobile Association, the sanctioning body that conducted the "500" and most other big-league racing in the U.S., opted

Drivers and crew members pose on the track for a 1952 pre-race photo.

Rookie Cecil Green, driving for Tulsa sportsman John Zink, is on his way to a fine 4th-place finish in 1950.

to stop doing so. Politicians, editors, even car makers, jumped on the anti-racing bandwagon.

All this was still ahead as Indianapolis prepared for the 1955 race. Vukovich was going for his third win in a row, and it seemed the whole world was watching.

Race day found an enormous crowd at the Speedway. Dinah Shore was there blowing kisses from the red and white Chevrolet Bel Air pace car. Tony Hulman, who had assumed Shaw's duties, uttered for his first time the most famous words in motorsport: "Gentlemen, start your engines."

Vuky, now driving for Atlanta businessman Lindsey Hopkins, batted the early lead back and forth with Jack McGrath. When McGrath dropped out on Lap 54, Vuky was alone at the front.

On the very next lap a melee erupted a little past the exit to Turn 2. And when it was all over, hard-

1955 Chevrolet Bel Air pace car driven by Chevrolet General Manager Tom Keating. Standing next to the car is three-time "500" winner Mauri Rose.

Minus almost all the streamlined bodywork it sported at the beginning of the month, Jimmy Daywalt's No. 48 Sumar Special is dicing with Pat Flaherty's No. 89 Dunn Engineering Special in the '55 "500."

nosed ironman Bill Vukovich, the personification of the Indianapolis 500 and a hero to school kids and old codgers alike, was dead.

Fifty-five years later, hardly a day goes by that a Speedway visitor taking the Hall of Fame Museum's bus tour of the track doesn't ask where, exactly, on the back stretch did Vuky's crash occur.

Italy's Alberto Ascari had been killed at Monza four days before Vuky. And on June 11, the terrible crash at Le Mans took more than 80 spectator lives. When the AAA announced August 3 that it was

Bob Sweikert holds a post-race _Indianapolis News_ front page moments after winning the 1955 race. Tony Hulman is on the left and TV star Dinah Shore on the right.

OFFICIAL PROGRAM

36th 500 MILE RACE

May 30, 1952

50c Pay No More . . . INDIANAPOLIS MOTOR SPEEDWAY CORPORATION

1952 program.

This is a quiz. Which of these Kurtis cars in the '53 race is a new KK5000 roadster? A clue: It's the one with the driver (Jim Rathmann) seated lower and the bodywork that comes up to his shoulders.

Troy Ruttman (left) and fellow driver Marshall Teague catch a snack and try to stay cool in 1954 after handing their cars over to relief drivers. The nice man holding the blanket is unidentified.

If you bought a $3 crash helmet at this open-air stand in 1951 you got a free pair of goggles.

done at the end of the year, Hulman organized the United States Auto Club. Since so many former AAA officials joined the USAC staff, perhaps the most noticeable difference between the organizations was the arm band.

Meanwhile, Vuky's good friend Bob Sweikert had won the 1955 race for Tulsa industrialist John Zink. His chief mechanic was a crewcut California kid named A.J. Watson, who would make frequent trips to Victory Lane in the years ahead as the winning car-builder. A number of top-notch car builders

1951 ticket.

1953 ticket.

1954 ticket.

1958 ticket.

1954 program.

The horrific first-lap melee in 1958 eliminated eight cars from the race and took the life of popular driver Pat O'Connor. Ed Elisian was driving the No. 5 car in the foreground. Rebuilt in less than 30 days, it was driven by Jim Rathmann at the Monza (Italy) 500. He won all three heats.

would do wonderful things with the Kurtis design in the coming years. But students of Indianapolis 500 history generally agree that if Frank Kurtis invented the roadster, Watson perfected it.

After the tragedies of 1955, the Speedway enjoyed a great race in '56. Fittingly, Jim Rathmann led the first three laps in the rebuilt Vukovich car. Driving a new Watson, popular Pat Flaherty won the pole with a new track record. He also won the race. The ride had gone to Flaherty when Sweikert quit the Zink team.

There were a lot of little things distinguishing the '56 Watson from the original Kurtis, but the big thing was the engine position. It was upright and scooted a full foot to the left of center. Since the Watson was super light, the left-side bias amounted to 16 percent of total car weight. And that translated into faster turn speeds.

Taking a completely different tack and with Quin Epperly's help, George Salih laid the engine almost completely on its side in a little car he hand-built at his California home. Money was tight, so Salih tried to sell the car. When he couldn't, he brought it to Indianapolis in 1957 and installed Sam Hanks as his driver.

Another huge Speedway crowd watched as Hanks and Paul Russo, driving a brutish Novi, played hare-and-hound: the biggest car in the "500" chasing the smallest. Hanks could pull ahead in the turns. But the Novi would be all over him on the straights. When the Novi finally faded, Hanks went on to take the checkered flag for Salih, who found himself suddenly and very unexpectedly $103,000 richer.

If you know this majorette was 5 foot 6, you get an idea of the size of Purdue's big base drum in 1957.

Jack McGrath, who started on the outside of the front row, has the lead as the field moves through Turn 1 in 1952.

Defending Indy champion Jimmy Bryan with his trademark cigar in 1959.

Eventual winner Jimmy Bryan, in George Salih's Belond Special, leads rookie George Amick by less than a car-length as the 1958 race winds down. Amick will finish second.

Johnny Boyd (No. 33), Jack Turner (No. 24) and Don Branson (No. 9) do battle in 1959.

Pit stops in the '50s weren't as choreographed as they are a half-century later. Tony Bettenhausen awaits service in 1956 as a car just ahead is pushed back into the fray.

Hanks had retired after '57 (he'd been named by Hulman as the "500's" director of racing), so Salih put three-time national champion Jimmy Bryan behind the wheel of his low-slung homebuilt car. Bryan managed to avoid the first-lap pile-up that took the life of his close friend Pat O'Connor to bring Salih his second win in a row.

Incidentally, Bryan had come from the Dean Van Lines team, which replaced him with a 23-year-old Texas rookie named A.J. Foyt.

Driver Jimmy Daywalt seems oblivious to the swirling mass of humanity immediately at his feet as he looks across a fence separating the garage area from the rest of the world on Race Day in 1959.

With only fourth gear left, Bobby Unser needs a strong push from his crew as he exits his pit late in the 1968 race. Inheriting the lead when Joe Leonard's turbine-powered STP car expired on Lap 191, Unser went on to win his first "500."

ENGINE! WHAT? WHERE?
1960-1969

❞The traditional Speedway fraternity had no idea how to combat the funny car invasion. The shortsighted among them ignored, or laughed at, the little cars. The more forward-looking recognized the danger, but were powerless to head it off.❞

— author Gary Wayne

Except for the Tucker Torpedo and Lou Fageol's twin-engine creation in 1946, and a couple of pre-war entries, every car that ever ran at Indianapolis through 1960 had its engine in front of the driver.

The ubiquitous roadster was merely the latest iteration. As the decade dawned at Indy, it was the only game in town. It wasn't a matter of

Dan Gurney

Dan Gurney's race driving and car building credentials are impeccable. But serious students of motor sport also view him as one of the founding fathers of the rear-engine revolution at Indianapolis. He introduced a reluctant Colin Chapman to the Indy scene in 1962 and brokered the deal that brought Ford to the "500" in 1963.

needing one to *win* Indy. You needed one to *race*. And nobody thought the situation would change anytime soon. Almost nobody, anyway.

It was the Speedway's Golden Anniversary era. Carl Fisher's ancient formula still worked: Huge purses plus a great show equals a sell-out crowd. The Speedway sold more than half-a-million tickets during May 1960, and race winner Jim Rathmann's share of the $369,000 purse was $110,000.

Numbers like that resonated with racers everywhere. One of them was Englishman John Cooper, who had befriended Indianapolis 500 champ Rodger Ward at the first (and only) U.S. Grand Prix road race at Sebring in December 1959. Ward was there racing his midget, of all things. Cooper was there with two little rear-engine cars bearing his name. Young Bruce McLaren was driving one. Jack Brabham, who would win the 1959 Formula One championship if he finished no worse than fourth, was in the other.

McLaren ended up winning the race when Brabham ran out of gas 400 yards shy of the checkered flag. Although he had the championship locked up anyway, Brabham pushed his car across the finish line.

Harlan Fengler behind the wheel of the 1963 Chrysler 30 pace car.

Ward was impressed. It took awhile, but he eventually persuaded Cooper of the car's potential for capturing a piece of that enormous Indy purse. The track was duly booked, and one of Cooper's Formula One cars shipped in.

On October 5, 1960, with Ward and other racers looking on, Jack Brabham turned it loose.

Andrew Ferguson, who was a Cooper manager at the time, wrote years later, "Right from its first laps, the knowledgeable onlookers were agog.

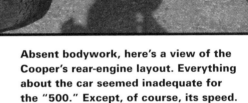

Absent bodywork, here's a view of the Cooper's rear-engine layout. Everything about the car seemed inadequate for the "500." Except, of course, its speed.

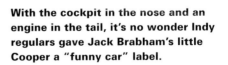

With the cockpit in the nose and an engine in the tail, it's no wonder Indy regulars gave Jack Brabham's little Cooper a "funny car" label.

The famous Cooper-Climax that started the rear engine revolution in 1961.

Smokey Yunick entered this "side car" in 1964. Bobby Johns crashed it as he was warming up for a qualifying run.

Andy Granatelli had a special chassis built for the helicopter turbine he bought to power Parnelli Jones' "Whoosh-mobile" in 1967.

Fred Agabashian won the 1952 pole position in this turbocharged Cummins Diesel. He was out of the race early because of an overheated engine caused by debris clogging the turbocharger. But turbocharging took hold at Indy by the late 1960s.

"WEIRD AND INNOVATIVE CARS"

Pat Clancy's tandem-axle six-wheel car was an effort in 1948 to gain speed with increased traction.

Joe Leonard's turbine-powered Lotus No. 60 seemed unbeatable in 1968.

That year's pole had been taken at 146.952 mph, and the race-winning average was 138.767, yet here was a 'foreigner' new to the track, driving a 'funny car' (the contemporary American term for a rear-engined car) with an undersized engine

Richard "Jim" Rathmann

When young Dick Rathmann swapped IDs with older brother Jim so he could enter a drag race in the early 1940s, nobody thought Dick would become Jim forevermore. But that's what happened. Thus it is that Jim Rathmann's name is on the Borg-Warner Trophy for winning one of the most thrilling Indianapolis 500s of all time. It was 1960, and, as spectators held their breath, Rathmann went side-by-side and nose-to-tail with defending "500" champ Rodger Ward through much of the last half of the race.

1.7 cc below the regulation limit, yet lapping at 144.834 mph!"

What was even more telling: Sticky tires and a sophisticated suspension permitted Brabham to run almost flat out all around the track. His corner speeds were in the low 140s—the fastest on record.

There was a new kid on the block.

Cooper quickly had a chassis strengthened and an engine bored and stroked to its maximum 2.75 liters. It made maybe 260 horsepower, two-thirds that of a standard-issue Offy. The total package weighed 1,200 pounds.

Then it was off to Indianapolis. Qualifying at 145.1 mph, Brabham was 13th on the grid. He finished ninth, which was pretty good considering his Dunlop tires wore a lot faster than the Firestones everyone else was using. And an unschooled Cooper pit crew took twice as long as the Americans to change them.

Most people viewed the "funny car" as a curiosity. A few, especially those who understood the significance of corner speeds fully eight miles an hour faster than anyone else, took it seriously.

Meanwhile, A.J. Foyt outran Eddie Sachs, both, of course, in Offy-powered roadsters, to notch his first Indianapolis win. It was worth almost $118,000 in purse money to the Bowes Seal Fast team.

On the surface, at least, nothing seemed wavering about the status quo. But the game changers were getting their act together. There was curt British driver Colin Chapman, for instance, the boss at Lotus Cars, doodling during lunch. There was Indy rookie Dan

Fifty years after the first "500," race day attire is a little more casual in 1961 than it was in 1911.

The portable cot and a big drink cooler in a little red wagon would suggest this is a veteran group of race fans, circa 1961.

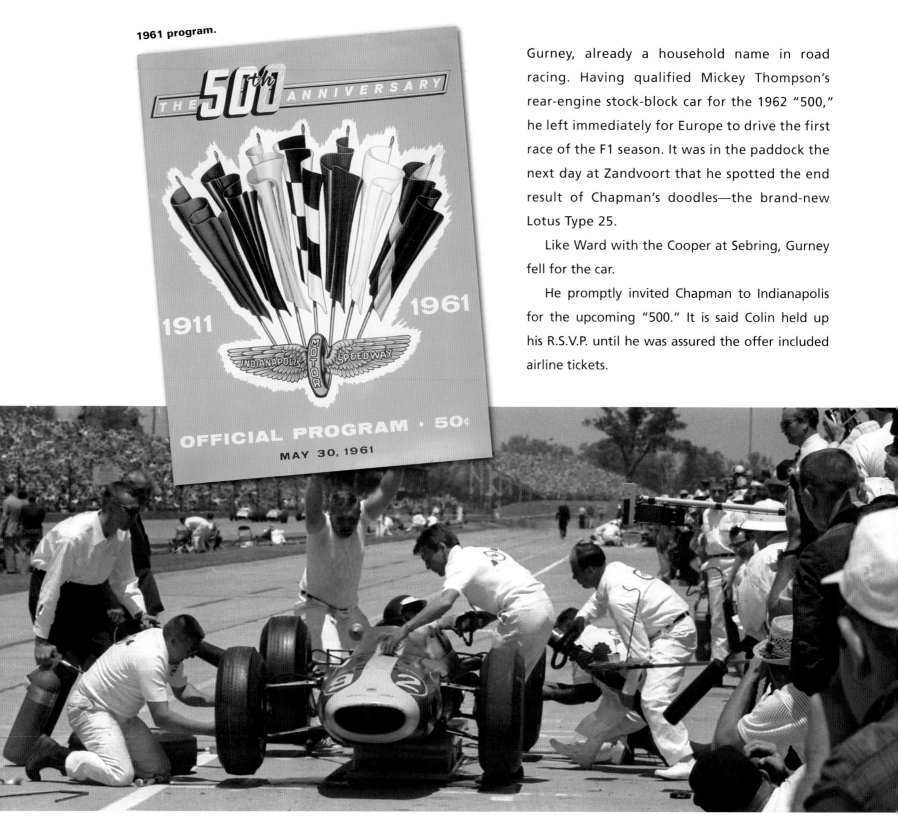

1961 program.

Gurney, already a household name in road racing. Having qualified Mickey Thompson's rear-engine stock-block car for the 1962 "500," he left immediately for Europe to drive the first race of the F1 season. It was in the paddock the next day at Zandvoort that he spotted the end result of Chapman's doodles—the brand-new Lotus Type 25.

Like Ward with the Cooper at Sebring, Gurney fell for the car.

He promptly invited Chapman to Indianapolis for the upcoming "500." It is said Colin held up his R.S.V.P. until he was assured the offer included airline tickets.

Jim Clark only made one pit stop in 1963, which was a good thing since his pit crew needed more than twice as long to service the car as a veteran American crew would typically take.

Then there were Ford Motor Co. engineers Don Frey and Dave Evans, who watched the '62 race (which Ward won) from the stands and talked on the way home about how Ford could lead the rear-engine revolution.

There was also Atlanta banker and long-time race car owner Lindsey Hopkins, who would say years later he knew the instant he saw the little Cooper that he was looking at the future of the "500."

All these forces came together in early July 1962, when Gurney and Chapman walked into the boardroom at Ford Headquarters in Dearborn, Michigan. There were many opinions about what happened that day. But no question the outcome was a Lotus/Ford alliance that would soon render the roadster obsolete.

You can tag 1963 as the year the tide turned. Mickey Thompson had two rear-engine stock-block cars in the race. But the true genesis cars of the Indianapolis 500's new era were new Lotus Type 29s driven by Gurney and Formula One star Jimmy Clark and powered by souped-up Ford passenger

1965 Plymouth Sports Fury pace car driven by P.M. Buckminster.

A.J. Foyt

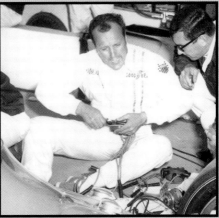

A.J. Foyt was the first driver to win the "500" four times. He holds the records for most consecutive and career starts (35), most races led (13), most times led (39), and most total laps and miles driven. As Kenny Brack's car owner, Foyt won a fifth "500" in 1999.

the 47th 500

INDIANAPOLIS MOTOR SPEEDWAY

OFFICIAL PROGRAM · 50¢

MAY 30, 1963

1963 program.

In this famous photo, Eddie Sachs strolls into the pits after the 1963 race with the wheel he lost in a crash after spinning in oil allegedly leaking from Parnelli Jones' winning car.

car engines. Clark finished second to Parnelli Jones in J.C. Agajanian's famous "Calhoun," a Watson roadster that escaped being black-flagged although it seemed to be losing oil as the race wound down.

With a full-scale funny car invasion under way in 1964, the introduction of the Ford four-cam engine, a tire war, lots of new hot shoes, and the first-ever live closed circuit telecast in place, the race promised excitement aplenty. What it delivered was a fiery second-lap pileup that took the lives of Eddie Sachs and Dave MacDonald.

There were 24 rear-engine cars entered in the '64 race, 12 of which made the grid. Parnelli tried one but opted to qualify "Calhoun" one more time. Foyt ended up going with his roadster, too.

Paul Goldsmith (No. 99) and Troy Ruttman (No. 17) do battle in 1963. Their engine layouts are at opposite extremes. That bulge in the side of Ruttman's Eddie Kuzma-built car hides the top end of an Offy, which is lying on its side. Thus, the lower hood line. The Offy in Goldsmith's A.J. Watson-built car is upright and offset to the left, which makes for a higher hood line but permits an overall narrower profile. Ruttman finished 12th, Goldsmith 18th.

J.C. Agajanian

One of Indy's most unforgettable characters, car owner J.C. Agajanian, wore big cowboy hats and boots made in Spain. From 1948 through 1971, his cars started on the pole three times, set four track records, and won the race twice.

Just as Bob Sweikert's win in '55 was overshadowed by Bill Vukovich's death, the awful '64 accident cast a pall over Foyt's second "500" victory. It would be the last for a roadster.

Amid the finger-pointing after the 1964 race, the United States Auto Club crossed a bridge. USAC had a splendid opportunity to outright ban rear-engine cars. It opted instead for a two-stage bump in minimum weight (1,250 pounds in '65, 1,350 in '66), which produced cries of pain from the roadster fraternity and relief from the funny car crowd. Then, it mandated sponge-filled fuel cells and a two pit-stop minimum for the "500." Since mileage now didn't matter as much, methanol instantly replaced highly volatile gasoline as the fuel of choice. And that's what USAC wanted all along.

Altogether, USAC actions left no doubt those funny cars were here to stay.

To the delight of an estimated 200,000 people at the Speedway for pole position qualifying in 1965, it seemed like new speed records were being set every few minutes. When the field was finally set,

Harlan Fengler circles the track in the 1968 Ford Torino pace car.

1960 ticket.

1963 ticket.

1969 program.

Jimmy Clark, A.J. Foyt and Parnelli Jones, three of Indy's greatest, were nose-to-tail in this classic photo of the 1965 race.

A brilliant practitioner of the art of getting noticed, car owner Andy Granatelli outfitted his pit crew in these eye-catching uniforms in 1967.

Andy Granatelli's two front-engine Novis were there along with two front-engine Watson roadsters, two Watson clones…and 27 rear engine cars.

Foyt was on the pole. Clark was next to him in a brand-new Lotus Type 35. With the Wood Brothers of NASCAR fame handling his pit stops, Clark settled into a 150 mph pace that left him almost alone on the lead lap as the checkered flag flew. Parnelli Jones finished second. Clark was pushed hard at the end by young Mario Andretti, whose great run made him Rookie of the Year.

Graham Hill was no stranger to racing, but in 1966, he was a first-timer at Indianapolis. He won the race for young Texas oilman John Mecom, but

Car owner Al Dean (center) and chief mechanic Clint Brawner (right) were already "500" legends in 1965. Mario Andretti (left), still a rookie, soon will be.

Despite this qualification day spin, Norm Hall earned a last-row starting position in 1961. He finished a fine 10th.

Rookie-of-the-Year honors went to his teammate, Jackie Stewart.

An internal combustion engine is essentially an air pump. The more air pumped in, the more power it makes. Since the 1920s, a belt driven off the crankshaft spun a fan that forced air into the combustion chambers of many racing

Modern era race fans associate No. 14 with A.J. Foyt. But in 1963, Roger McCluskey drove No. 14 and Foyt drove No. 2. Foyt finished third, which is where McCluskey was running until he spun with just two laps to go.

Mario Andretti

Mario Andretti started 29 Indy's and finished just nine, including the 1969 race, which he won. He broke Indy's 200-mph barrier during practice in 1977. His last "500" as a driver was 1994.

Dan Gurney (left) and
Jackie Stewart in 1967.

GOOD⁄EAR

Fire

engines at Indy. Supercharging, they callled it. But turbocharging—where exhaust air takes the place of a belt—was an untried science until engine builder Herb Porter bolted one to a spare Offy in late '65.

It was a last-resort effort to save the Offy from extinction.

When the device got him an amazing 200 more horsepower, he called in ageless Leo Goosen to completely redesign the engine. They ended up

Eddie Sachs (No. 12), Don Branson (No. 3), and Jim Hurtubise (No. 99) make up the front row in 1961. For years, the racing fraternity made the Holiday Inn across 16th Street from the Speedway one of its unofficial headquarters.

Driving a Ford-powered Coyote, Joe Leonard started fifth and finished third in 1967.

Ford engines didn't take as easily to turbocharging as the Offys did in the late '60s, so mechanics tried various things to make them more efficient. The ductwork on George Follmer's No. 62 car was one effort. He started 27th in 1969 and finished 27th.

The fueling process is intense and arduous as Bobby Unser pits on his way to winning the 1968 race.

Joe Leonard was on the pole in this turbine-powered stub-tail Lotus in 1968. He finished 12th. That fellow in the sport coat by the right front tire is car owner Andy Granatelli.

with a short-stroke, high-revving 2.8-liter package that saw action for the first time at the "500" in 1966, when Bobby Unser finished eighth.

The turbo bandwagon was rolling. But it was an even more radical idea that fixated the racing world in 1967: the turbine. Parnelli Jones ran off and left everyone in Andy Granatelli's wide, red STP machine. He was ahead of A.J. Foyt by 43 seconds on the 197th lap when the failure of a $6 transmission bearing put him out of the race.

Andy returned in 1968 with three turbines wrapped in wedge-shaped Lotus bodywork. Joe Leonard put one on the pole with a track record of 171.95. As he resumed speed after a late-race caution, his engine flamed out. A broken fuel shaft was blamed. The same thing happened at about

Twenty-three years after he and his brothers first entered a car in the "500," Andy Granatelli finally made it to Victory Lane in 1969 with Mario Andretti. The picture of exuberant Andy giving Mario a big kiss made newspapers around the world.

Seconds after this photo of the start of the '66 race was taken, a chain reaction crash in Turn 1 took out 11 cars.

Graham Hill (No. 24) and Jackie Stewart (No. 43) were both newcomers to the "500" in 1966. Hill won the race and Stewart, who led 40 of the last 50 laps, was named Rookie of the Year.

the same time to the other turbine still running at the time, and Bobby Unser picked up the win. And yes, his Offy-powered Eagle was turbocharged. It was another "500" first.

After so many close calls, Granatelli brothers Andy, Joe, and Vince finally made it to Victory Lane in 1969. The classic photo of Andy in Victory Lane planting a huge kiss on Mario Andretti's cheek says it all.

It was Pole Day in 1969 and rookie Jigger Sirois (shown here in a 1974 photo) was on a 161.5 mph qualifying run. Thinking it wasn't fast enough, his crew called him in. Then the rains came. The day ended with no qualifiers, and Sirois never made the race.

In the '70s, the underside of a wing was top-secret territory, so this is a rare view. Notice how far the wing sticks out behind the car.

THE WING'S THE THING
1970-1979

❝At the Indianapolis 500, anything is possible. If you can avoid potential catastrophes, you will be successful. This takes experience, steady nerves, and attention to both detail and attitude. Maybe even more than that, it takes luck, if not divine intervention.❞

Tom Binford, chief steward

I f you chart pole position qualifying speeds at Indianapolis you will find they only increased an average 1.5 miles per hour per year through the first six decades. That's right: From around 80 mph to 170. And despite the abruptness of rule changes and technical breakthroughs with machinery and the track, the trend line is eerily uniform.

Bobby Unser

Bobby Unser won three Indianapolis 500s ('68, '75 and '81) during a career that began in 1963 and included 19 starts.

Then you come to 1971. The gentle upward curve goes stratospheric.

The stage had actually been set in the late 1960s, which saw more performance progress than ever before at the "500." Credit the transition to rear-mounted engines, four-wheel independent suspension, much wider wheels, more advanced high-traction tires, and a growing awareness of how the movement of air around a race car affected its performance.

Colin Chapman's wedge-shaped 1968 STP-Lotus turbines were an early attempt to create downforce with minimum drag at racing speeds. A few cars showed up in 1969 with little winglets ahead of the front wheels and ducktail bodywork in the rear. The first crude rear wings appeared in 1970.

That was the year Topper Toys sponsored the car Vel Miletich and Parnelli Jones commissioned George Bignotti to build for Al Unser. When Unser won from the pole (he led 190 laps), the exposure made the little blue and yellow Johnny Lightning model an instant collector item and introduced a great many kids to Indy cars.

Although the car was different, the same team would win in 1971. But in the run-up to the race, the name on the lips of race fans wasn't Johnny Lightning. It was Bruce McLaren. The New Zealander had been killed during testing at Goodwood just months before, but his company had three new cars for Indy. Two were for Peter Revson and Dennis Hulme. Roger Penske entered the other for Mark Donohue.

Designed by Gordon Coppuck, the McLaren was a another game changer.

This Johnny Lightning scale model of Al Unser's 1970 winner was a surprise best-seller for Topper Toys, which sponsored Al's 1970/'71 winners. Mint-condition originals are very rare. If you're Mike Delporte of Indianapolis, you are the proud owner of not just this '70 car, but a boxed '71. It's never been opened.

1970 AL UNSER JOHNNY LIGHTNING® SPECIAL™

Al Unser, in the famous Johnny Lightning car No. 2, led all but 10 laps on his way to his first "500" win.

"THE HALL OF FAME MUSEUM"

No visit to the Speedway is complete without a stop at the 96,000 square-foot Hall of Fame Museum. Since only a fraction of the museum's properties can be displayed at any one time, exhibits are changed frequently. Here are A.J. Foyt's four winning cars.

It was longer and carefully packaged to produce a very low polar moment of inertia. The engine was mostly ahead of the rear wheel centerline, not behind it. And rather than a stubby appendage that acted more like a spoiler, it had a real rear wing with the underside designed to create a low-pressure zone.

At first glance, the wing didn't appear to be integrated into the bodywork of the car, which was a USAC requirement. But Coppuck persuaded inspectors that the structure to which his wing was bolted was actually the engine cover. Acting like an inverted airplane wing, it produced more than 600 pounds of aerodynamic downforce at 200 mph, nearly half the static weight of the car.

With that much force pressing down on his car, Donohue practiced at 4 mph faster through the corners than anybody had ever gone before. On Thursday before Pole Day, with a top speed at the end of the straights of nearly 220 mph, he unofficially broke Indy's 180-mph barrier.

The 1970 Oldsmobile 442 pace car.

Of the non-McLarens, A.J. Foyt was fastest at 175.3.

Donohue's four-lap qualifying run put him on the pole with a new track record. But at under 178 mph, it was slower than expected. A disappointed Donohue apparently mentioned to Revson a few

Al Unser Sr.

Beginning in 1965, Al Unser Sr. started 27 Indys. He won four, including the 1987 race, when he was a last-minute replacement for injured Danny Ongais in a car that had graced a hotel lobby in Pennsylvania just a few days earlier.

minutes later that certain chassis adjustments had not been made to his car. Revson, who was in line to qualify, quickly incorporated the changes to his McLaren. Soon thereafter, he dislodged Mark from the pole with his own record run of 178.69—a breathtaking eight miles an hour faster than Al Unser's speed the year before.

Donohue, who had finished second in 1970, was out front and running strong in 1971 until his transmission broke on Lap 66. Unser and Vel's Parnelli teammate Joe Leonard entertained the sellout crowd for the next 55 laps, swapping the lead time and again. Then Leonard's turbocharger soured, and Unser went on to become only the fourth driver in Speedway history to win back-to-back "500s." It was his 32nd birthday.

Speedway soothsayers thought 1972 would be a catch-your-breath year after the burst of speed in '71. They couldn't have been more mistaken.

If caution is a virtue with the management of venerable institutions such as the "500," it's probably okay to suggest that USAC threw it to the winds in 1972. New rules liberalized wing size, shape, and placement. The effect was something to behold.

Pole Day in 1972 saw an estimated 200,000 people at the track. As they gasped in disbelief, the first three qualifiers each set new one and four-lap records. Then came Al Unser's older brother Bobby in one of Dan Gurney's new Eagles.

His four-lap average was 195.940, a staggering seven miles an hour faster than the fastest of the first three, and 17 faster than Revson's '71 pole speed. Never in the history of the "500" had a qualifying record been so handily dispatched.

David Hobbs (No. 68) was already fairly well known in international road racing, but he was a rookie at Indianapolis in 1971. That's Bentley Warren (No. 95) running alongside him.

Mark Donohue (No. 66) has the inside line on Sam Sessions (No. 52) as the 1972 race winds down. Donohue takes the win. Sessions who started 24th, is 4th.

1972 program.

In 1972, the wing was "the thing" when it came to the application of downforce on a race car. Optimizing front and rear wings, Bobby Unser set a new qualifying record in this Olsonite Eagle. Ignition failure ended his race early.

Movie and TV star James Garner, a long-time "500" insider, drove the Oldsmobile pace car in 1977.

Jim Hurtubise

Jim Hurtubise took the green flag in only 10 Indys and never finished higher than 13th (1962), but to the "500" crowd of the '60s and '70s, he was a most likeable maverick. He was a rookie and a final-day qualifier in 1960, when he electrified a crowd of 80,000 with a four-lap run of 149.056 mph. That was a tick beneath the elusive 150 mph mark and an incredible 2.5 mph faster than Eddie Sachs' pole position speed. Hurtubise is also well remembered for a 1972 stunt. That's when he replaced the engine in his Miller High Light Special with five cases of his sponsor's product and passed it around on pit row after qualifying ended.

1977 Oldsmobile Delta 88 pace car with passengers Tony Hulman and A.J. Foyt riding on roof.

Chief mechanic George Bignotti (left) and a young Johnny Capels wait with Joe Leonard for the start of the 1972 race. Leonard finished third.

At 200 miles an hour, the downforce generated by the front and rear wings of Jim Hurtubise's Coyote almost doubled the static weight of the car in 1972.

Mario Andretti's No. 9 Viceroy Parnelli bristled with wings and winglets at the start of practice in 1972, but many were quickly removed once practice began. In the race, he ran out of fuel with five laps to go.

Gordon Johncock

Gordon Johncock competed in 24 Indys and won twice. While his 1973 win was overshadowed by the miserable weather and several crashes, his 1982 win over Rick Mears was a splendid polar opposite. Under ideal racing conditions, Johncock held off Mears in the closing laps to win by .16 seconds.

Buried in the details of Unser's historic run, however, were the seeds of the next big aerodynamic adventure at Indianapolis.

Unser's best straightaway speed was 206 mph. Under the old rules a year earlier, Donohue saw 216-plus on his qualifying run. So you had the bizarre situation of Unser running the straights 10 mph slower but actually completing the lap a good 15 mph faster than Donohue.

The same big wings that aided Unser's corner speeds slowed him down on the straights. The conundrum tantalized the deep thinkers. How do you lose drag without sacrificing downforce? And what might that do to your lap time? The answer, of course, was "ground effects." And Indy's car-builders were soon on it.

Meanwhile, the 1972 race sported what was, by far, the fastest front row in Indianapolis history: Bobby Unser, Revson, and Donohue. Mechanical failures took Revson and Unser out early. Gary Bettenhausen had his McLaren up front for much of the rest of the race, but when starter Pat Vidan hauled out the checkered flag, it was Donohue

Racing veteran Jackie Stewart behind the wheel of the 1979 Ford Mustang pace car.

there to take it. Car owner Roger Penske had his first "500" win.

With speeds rising so far so fast, an official 200 mph lap at Indianapolis seemed just around the corner. Veteran Johnny Rutherford came within two tenths of a second on the third lap of his qualifying run in 1973. Nobody would run faster until 1977.

What a lot of people remember about the mid-70s at Indianapolis is the weather. Tom Binford, chief

1972 ticket.

Attending the 1972 race as a guest of Bill Harrah, TV star Jim Nabors was surprised when Tony Hulman asked him Race Day morning to "sing the song." Thinking Hulman meant the National Anthem, Nabors said "okay." When he learned he would be doing "Back Home Again in Indiana," he wrote the words on his hand. His rendition, without rehearsal, brought a hushed crowd of 350,000 to its feet. He's been singing it almost every year since then. Here he sings in 1974.

1973 ticket.

MONDAY, MAY 28, 1973
57th ★ 500 MILE
International Sweepstakes

MARK DONOHUE ★ 1972 WINNER

Admission to Grounds
1973
THE INDIANAPOLIS MOTOR SPEEDWAY CORP.

This Coupon good for Gate Admission to grounds only

NOT GOOD IF DETACHED

GATE ADMISSION $5.00

NASCAR ace Bobby Allison (right) drove for Roger Penske in 1973. His engine expired on the first lap.

steward from 1974 to '95, often said that had it not rained three days in a row in '73, his predecessor would still have the job.

In 1974, the Arab oil embargo prompted a cutback in allotted qualifying time. Then, it rained. The six teams still in line when time trials ended quickly took legal action. The suit they filed was dismissed a couple of days later.

The 1975 race ended in a downpour so sudden that several cars spun before they could get slowed down.

Rain stopped the 1976 race on the 103rd lap. When they finally called it after a lengthy delay and another shower, Johnny Rutherford became the first "500" winner in history to walk into Victory Circle. It was also the shortest race in Speedway history.

The rain gods relented in 1977, and Indianapolis enjoyed a spectacular sun-splashed "500." The starting field included Tom Sneva, who had broken the 200-mile per hour barrier in qualifying; Janet Guthrie, the first woman to make the race; five former winners; and three sets of siblings. At the end, it was A.J. Foyt in Victory Circle.

Tony Hulman died in October 1977, a month shy of 32 years after his purchase of the track saved it from extinction. Five months later, a plane crash took the lives of eight key USAC officials. Long festering issues, mainly over the size of the purses at other USAC races on the Championship trail, came to a head in November. Team owners organized Championship Auto Racing Teams (aka CART) and announced a calendar of CART races for 1979.

When USAC refused entries involving 19 CART cars for the 1979 "500," the teams went to court.

Their request for an injunction was granted and they were allowed in. For the next 15 years, the "500" found CART and USAC in uneasy co-existence.

INDY PROFILE

George Bignotti

At one point in George Bignotti's many-faceted life, he was a San Francisco florist. His first trip to Indianapolis as a bona-fide race crew member was in 1954. With 85 victories (including seven "500s") over the next 30 years, he would become the winningest chief mechanic in Indycar history.

These drivers were all rookies in 1974. (Left to right) Tom Sneva, who would win the 1983 race, Pancho Carter, Bill Simpson, Jan Opperman, Tom Bigelow, Larry Cannon, and Johnny Parsons.

1976 program.

Comedian Bob Hope was on hand for the 1976 race.

Already proclaimed the Racing Capital of the World, the hallowed Speedway property made the National Register of Historic Places in 1975.

1977 ticket.

1977 program.

Grounds superintendent Clarence Cagle and Speedway owner Tony Hulman in 1977. Cagle will soon retire. Hulman will pass away in October.

Young Rick Mears shares a moment with his car owner, Roger Penske, before the 1979 race. Mears will start (and win) from the pole. It would be his first "500" win, Penske's second.

Flesh tone seems to be the most popular color on Race Day in 1977.

Mario Andretti (No. 7) goes low in Turn 1 as he races with Mike Mosley (No. 78) in 1978.

By 1978, it seemed the entire car was a wing. Gordon Johncock's No. 20 North American Van Lines is an example. He finished third.

"WOMEN DRIVERS AT THE INDY 500"

Thirty-five Indys after Janet Guthrie's first attempt to qualify, women drivers in the "500" field constitute a very exclusive club. In addition to Guthrie, who earned a starting spot in 1977, only six women have made the race. Three of them—Lyn St. James, Danica Patrick, and Simona de Silvestro—were named Rookie of the Year.

Janet Guthrie, an aerospace engineer before she began racing automobiles professionally, was the first woman to race in the "500" (1977).

Lyn St. James was rookie of the year at the 1992 "500." She's a veteran of seven Indys.

Sarah Fisher was 19 in 2000, when she qualified for her first "500." She formed her own team in 2008.

Danica Patrick's first "500" was in 2005, when she qualified 4th and led 19 laps on the way to finishing 4th. Starting 23rd in 2010, she led the race briefly before finishing 6th.

Milka Duno caught the racing bug during a visit to a driver's school in her native Venezuela when she was 24.

Brazilian road racer Ana Beatriz Caselato Gomes de Figueiredo started and finished 21st in 2010. It was her first "500."

Swiss-born Simona de Silvestro's 14th place finish in the 2010 "500" earned her Rookie of the Year honors.

If Jim Hall's 1979 Chaparral introduced full ground effects to Indianapolis, his '80 car refined the concept. Inside those pods were carefully designed tunnels, with the track surface as the floor. Johnny Rutherford put this car in Victory Lane.

THE AGE OF REFINEMENT
1980-1989

So until next May, this is Sid Collins, the voice of the 500, wishing you good morning, good afternoon and a good evening, depending on where in the world you are right now. We are here at the Indianapolis Motor Speedway, at the crossroads of America. Goodbye.

Sid Collins signing off, 1976

t's doubtful anybody would fuss much with a claim that Texan Jim Hall's Chaparral was to the 1980s at Indianapolis what the McLaren was to the '70s.

Hall's radical ground effects cars were the scourge of big league road racing in America before he turned his attention to the "500" in 1978. His Indy car that year was a reworked Lola and his driver was Al Unser, who would not only win the "500" but the Ontario and Pocono 500s, too.

Tom Sneva (No. 5) on his way to winning the 1983 race.

Nine-time Indy veteran Tom Bigelow will finish 8th in 1980.

"Spin-and-win" Danny Sullivan (No. 5) will soon pass Mario Andretti (No. 3) to take the 1985 victory.

Al Unser (No. 25) was tapped by a spinning Josele Garza (No. 55), then found himself a lap down early in the 1987 race. But when Mario Andretti fell out and Roberto Guerrero stalled in the pits, Unser was there to capture his fourth Indy win.

Johnny Rutherford

John Sherman Rutherford III, (aka Lone Star J.R.), who would win three "500s," was the boy wonder of NASCAR when he made his Indianapolis debut in 1963. Johnny won a 100-mile qualifying race for legendary Smokey Yunick in a Chevy powered by the infamous 427 cid "mystery engine." But it would be 10 years before he found Victory Lane at the "500." He won again in 1976, and again in 1980. He retired as a driver before the 1994 season.

But it was the '79 car, which was refined for '80, that really raised the bar. This one he designed with John Barnard and had custom built in England. Aside from its Pennzoil yellow paint, what set the car apart were the fat pods filling the space between front and rear wheels on each side.

Other cars had sidepods. That's where they tucked radiators, fuel tanks and the like. But none were as massive, or as empty. A close look at the Hall-Barnard creation revealed a solid fiberglass top, an open bottom, and sides so tight to the track that light hardly got through. Inside, there was nothing but an organically shaped underwing that utilized air movement from a miniscule slot in front through a mammoth hole in back to create a vacuum condition. True ground effects, they called it, the ultimate solution to the downforce vs. drag conundrum.

Despite teething problems, Unser qualified on the front row in 1979. He dominated the first half of the race, only to succumb to a bearing failure soon thereafter. Rick Mears ended up with the win, his first, and the second for car owner Roger Penske. A.J. Foyt coasted three-fourths of a lap with a dead engine to a second-place finish just a couple of seconds ahead of a hard-charging Mike Mosley.

A year later, almost everybody had a ground effects car. The Eagle Dan Gurney built for Mike Mosley took the concept to the furthest extreme. Sidepods were mounted astride rear axle halfshafts and extended behind the car.

But Hall's Chaparral, now driven by fellow Texan Johnny Rutherford, won the pole and the race. It was Rutherford's third win and the second in three years for Hall.

With 200 mph laps sprouting like dandelions in spring, the 1981 race promised excitement. It delivered in spades. Bobby Unser took the checkered flag but was later penalized a lap for advancing his position during a caution period. When the win was given to Mario Andretti, who had started 32nd and finished behind Unser, an appeal was filed. Six months later, USAC upheld

Genial John Cooper, USAC's first employee in 1955, was a senior Coke executive in 1979 when he was asked to assume the presidency of the Speedway. His appointment, coming as it did amidst the stressful early days of the USAC/CART split, made him a lightning rod. He later became president of Daytona International Speedway.

"INDY CELEBRITIES"

From its earliest days, the "500" has attracted big names in business, sports, politics, and entertainment. From Henry Ford and Harvey Firestone to Lance Armstrong to Presidents Reagan, Bush, and Clinton to Jack Nicholson, it's a star-studded celebrity roster.

Aviator Amelia Earhart in 1935.

One tradition that didn't last: Making casts of celebrity hand and footprints.

Clark Gable and Barbara Stanwyck in 1950, during the filming of *To Please a Lady*.

That's Marie Wilson of *My Friend Irma* TV fame between Roy Rogers (right) and James Melton, the opera singer (left), at a driver's meeting.

Wilbur Shaw (right) with Jack Benny in the cockpit and sidekick "Rochester" (left).

Singer, TV star Dinah Shore in 1955.

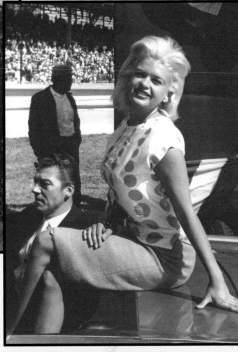
Jayne Mansfield and husband Mickey Hargitay.

Dancer Cyd Charisse rides with the Borg-Warner Trophy.

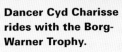
That's Johnny Carson of the *Tonight Show* behind those goggles.

Paul Newman stars in the Victory Lane scene in the movie *Winning*.

Indianapolis native David Letterman is part owner of a race team.

the appeal. And Unser's car owner, Roger Penske, had his third "500" championship.

Gordon Johncock, winner of the rain-shortened 1973 race, won again in '82, nipping Rick Mears at the checkered flag by just .16 seconds. With the official purse topping $2 million for the first time, Johncock's cut was $290,600.

Dan Gurney, the youngster who paid Colin Chapman's way to Indianapolis in 1962, who twice finished second at the "500," who unknowingly started a tradition when he sprayed the crowd in the winner's circle at Le Mans in '67 with champagne, who had been a driver or team owner at the "500" for 19 years, watched this one from the sidelines.

Also missing was Jim Hall's Chaparral team. The chassis of choice now was the British-built March. In addition to its customer cars, March mounted a full-bore factory effort with an Italian rookie named Teo Fabi, who promptly qualified on the pole.

Cigar-chomping Carl Haas announced he had talked actor Paul Newman into a race team partnership. Newman, a veteran sports car driver, said he asked Haas why in the world he should do such a thing. And Carl replied with two words: "Mario Andretti."

Twenty-one-year-old Al Unser Jr., (aka "Little Al") made the field along with his dad, "Big Al," and Indy had its first father-son combo. Late in the race, Little Al, who was down several laps at the time, got between his dad and Tom Sneva. Dad was leading. Sneva was coming on strong. As the crowd of an estimated 300,000 roared with delight, Little Al did what he could to hinder Sneva's progress. But all was for naught. Sneva, who had finished second three times, passed them both on Lap 191, and never looked back. He won by 10 seconds.

INDY PROFILE

Tom Binford

Indianapolis civic leader Tom Binford's D.A. Lubricants company sponsored race cars in the "500." He was a bank director, an interim head of DePaul University, and USAC president. Appointed chief steward after the 1973 race, he managed the "500" for the next 22 years.

Tom Binford
CHIEF STEWARD

OFFICIAL 1980 PROGRAM $3

64th ANNUAL

INDIANAPOLIS 500

PACE CAR
SWEEPSTAKES:

**Win a
Turbocharged
Pontiac
Trans Am**

Details Inside

CAR & DRIVER
LISTINGS

PONTIAC

1980 program.

**Like a flame attracts
a moth, a mud bog
in the infield in 1980
lured this hardy duo.**

Tom Sneva prepares for combat in 1983.

Al Unser Jr. has just touched wheels with Emerson Fittipaldi with a lap to go in the 1989 race.

Gordon Johncock ahead of Rick Mears by .16 second at the end of the 1982 race.

1981 program.

OFFICIAL PROGRAM $3.00

65TH INDIANAPOLIS 500

MAY 24th, 1981

1983 Buick Riviera pace car driven by Duke Nalon.

In a scene repeated many times at the "500," Mario Andretti (No. 12) and Bobby Unser (No.11) are nearly side by side at the start of the 1980 race.

When the Ford Motor Co. returned to racing in the 1960s, it didn't limit itself to U.S. venues. British drivers Mike Costin and Keith Duckworth were set up in business to build a world-beater Formula One engine. They were immensely successful. By the mid-'70s, not long after Ford pulled the plug on its in-house four-cam program, the first turbocharged version of the Cosworth Formula One engine found its way to Indianapolis. Tagged the DFX, it was more compact, more powerful, and more expensive than either the Offy or Ford's home-grown four-camer.

By the mid-'80s, the Cosworth was as dominant at the "500" as the Miller had been in the '20s or the Offy through the mid-century. The Cosworth/March was just about the only way to go. There were 30 on the Indy grid for 1984, and that was the combo Rick Mears drove to the win. It was his second, Roger Penske's fourth.

But the tide was turning.

The Andretti connection that attracted Newman to Haas also included Lola cars, another

1987 Chrysler LeBaron pace car.

Rick Mears

Rick Mears is one of only three racers to have won the "500" four times (1979, 1984, 1988, and 1991). Mears began racing on off-road tracks and made his transition to Indy car racing in the late 1970s. He suffered serious leg injuries in a 1984 crash in Quebec, Canada, racing at the Sanair track. He struggled some with the injuries but came back to win the "500" twice more before retiring in 1992.

1981 ticket.

It's party time in the Turn 1 area known as the Snake Pit in 1981.

British chassis builder. As the 1984 CART season progressed, Andretti and Danny Sullivan, both driving Lolas, collected eight wins between them. Andretti won the CART championship. It wouldn't be long before Lola would threaten March's near-monopoly at the "500."

On the engine front, engineers Mario Illien and Paul Morgan, both former employees at Cosworth, had a few good ideas and the gumption to make a late night trans-Atlantic call to Penske. That's what triggered the October 13, 1984, agreement between their young company and General Motors to build a new Indy race engine. Badged as a Chevrolet, the Ilmor was dyno-tested for the first time May 16, 1985.

Meanwhile, at Indy, it was the year of the spin-and-win. Danny Sullivan, the one-time New York cab driver, did his famous 360-degree spin on Lap 120, seconds after passing Andretti in Turn 1. Pitting for tires, he got back around Andretti in the same spot a few laps later, and went on to win the race. Penske had his fifth "500" victory.

The 1986 race was the first where the purse exceeded $4 million and the first to be televised live by ABC. The Greatest Spectacle in Racing became a spectacle in rain. Washed out twice

Emerson Fittipaldi

Brazilian Emerson Fittipaldi decided as a teenager that motorcycles and hydrofoils were too dangerous, so he began racing automobiles instead. Retiring in 1980 after a 10-year career in Formula One, he was back behind the wheel in 1984 as part of Pat Patrick's CART team. He won the 500 in 1989 after a late-race touch that found Al Unser Jr. spinning into the wall. He won again in 1993 with Penske.

and eventually run the following Saturday, Bobby Rahal won after slipping under Kevin Cogan on a restart with two laps to go.

An ailing Jim Trueman, the well-liked Ohio sportsman who owned Rahal's Truesports team, was able to take a victory lap in a bright yellow Corvette pace car. Eleven days later, he passed away.

Meanwhile, development of the Ilmor/Chevy engine was continuing. On November 17, as a few Chevrolet executives held their collective breath, Mears wheeled a Chevy-powered March around Michigan International Speedway to a new closed-course world record of 233.934 mph.

To the chagrin of officials, the glee of mechanics, and the giddy disbelief of spectators, Indianapolis saw a near-60 mph increase in lap speeds during the '70s and '80s. It was as if new rules intended to slow cars down had the opposite effect.

The focus on horsepower reduction in the early '80s was neutralized by ground effects and sticky tires. A 30 percent downforce reduction in 1986 was supposed to keep speeds well below 215 mph. The first lap of Mears' pole position qualifying

Test pilot Chuck Yeager piloted this 1988 Oldsmobile Cutlass pace car.

Like a racehorse in its stable, Tom Sneva's No. 5 Texaco Star awaits its date with destiny from behind the narrow wooden doors of Indy's ancient garages in 1983. Sneva won the race.

Al Unser Sr. (No. 1) and Al Unser Jr (No. 3) are nose-to-tail in 1988.

Danny Ongais would survive this terrible 1981 crash to race again at the "500."

Ken Hamilton didn't make the race in this very cab-forward Chevy-powered car in 1982.

run that year was a 217.581, and with the lighter, slimmer, more powerful Chevy V8 in the wings, Indianapolis hadn't seen anything yet.

In addition to the Penske team, both Newman-Haas and Patrick Racing were permitted to lease the

Rookie Al Unser Jr. (No. 19) who is several laps down, admits afterward that keeping between his dad and Tom Sneva (No. 5) was an objective in the closing laps of the 1983 race. Sneva eventually got around both Unsers and went on to capture the win. Notice the difference in sidepod configuration on these two cars.

Johnny Rutherford and Mario Andretti, two of Indy's most enduring stars, remain prominent on the "500" scene.

When Johnny Parsons spun in 1983, Mario Andretti (car 3) tried to go around the outside. He didn't quite make it.

1988 ticket.

1989 ticket.

Chevy for 1987. N-H's Mario Andretti put his Chevy/ Lola on the pole. He was cruising comfortably in front with 22 laps to go when his engine quit. And as the crowd groaned, legendary P.A. announcer Tom Carnegie uttered the words he'd used so often before to describe hard-luck Andretti's exit from competition: "Heeeee's sloooowing down."

Roberto Guerrero now led, but he soon pitted. The stop was lengthy, and veteran Al Unser, subbing for injured Danny Ongais and down a lap in a recently resurrected show car, found himself in the lead. He'd come to Indianapolis without a ride, and left a four-time "500" winner.

The track's racing surface was repaved before the 1988 race, so speeds were expected to rise. Teo Fabi was back with a Porsche factory effort, the first by a German firm since Mercedes in 1923. The Chevy ranks swelled with the addition of Rick Galles' Team Valvoline.

Mears laid down a 220-plus lap in practice. Andretti soon followed with a 221-plus. Mears trumped that with a 222.827. When everybody went to their qualifying setups, speeds fell off a tad. But at the end of Pole Day, it was an all-Penske, all-Chevy front row: Mears, Sullivan, Al Unser.

1985 program.

Twenty-three years after he was a rookie at the Brickyard, Parnelli Jones is still smiling in 1984.

Mears won the race from the pole. Jim Crawford, still limping from an awful crash in '87, was the only non-Penske driver to lead the race. His sixth-place finish with a stock-block Buick V6 engine was a valiant effort.

"Spin and win" became part of the Indy lexicon when Danny Sullivan did a 360 a couple of seconds after passing Mario Andretti for the lead in 1985. Pitting for tires, he passed Mario again 20 laps later in virtually the same place. That time, he made it stick.

Those huge openings on each side of the transaxle on Johnny Rutherford's No. 4 Chaparral in 1980 were part of the ground effects system.

Here are Indianapolis 500 winners Rick Mears, A.J. Foyt, Al Unser Sr., and Johnny Rutherford in 1989.

Brazil's famed Emerson Fittipaldi, who had been recruited to Formula One in 1970 by none other than Colin Chapman, won Indy in 1989. Racing side-by-side through Indy's treacherous corners, "Emmo" and Al Unser Jr. touched wheels on the 199th lap. Unser was sent spinning, but since the pair had a six-lap lead on the third place car, he was awarded second place. For the first time, the winner's share of the Indy purse was more than a million dollars.

To Emerson Fittipaldi's delight, the winner's share of the Indianapolis 500 purse topped a million dollars for the first time in 1989.

IMS chief Joe Cloutier (left) with Rick Mears (center) and Roger Penske (right) in Victory Lane in 1988.

Jim Crawford (No. 34) and Rick Mears (No. 2) race through the north chute in 1985.

Dale Coyne, who didn't make the race with this car in 1988, later became a car owner and a wizard at developing young talent.

Young Tony Stewart, the hottest shoe in USAC's midget and sprint car circuits, is a rookie at Indianapolis in 1996. Driving car No. 20, a dayglo yellow and orange Buick-powered car for retailing magnate John Menard, he starts on the pole and leads 44 of the first 55 laps. Engine failure on Lap 82 relegates him to a 24th-place finish.

THE CHANGING OF THE GUARD
1990-1999

I t would be correct to say change was in the air as the '90s dawned at Indianapolis. But that would not begin to describe the goings-on.

Joe Cloutier, who would often introduce himself as "just a bean counter" but was so much more, had been in charge at the Speedway for most of the 15 years before he died in December, 1989. A month later, Tony Hulman's grandson, 30-year-old Tony George, assumed the presidency.

Arie Luyendyk

Dutchman Arie Luyendyk, Rookie of the Year at Indianapolis in 1985, holds two Indy speed records that will be hard to break. He won the "500" in 1990 with an average speed of 185.981 mph. And he set a qualifying record of 237.498 mph in 1996. He won the 1997 race from the pole over Treadway Racing teammate Scott Goodyear. Retired from full-time racing after the 1999 season, he came back to drive in 2001 and 2002.

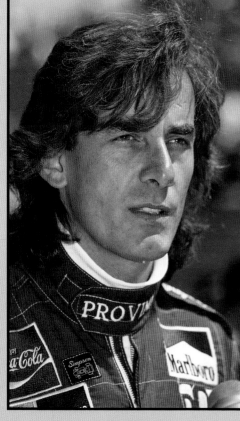

The tenuous situation was reminiscent of 1979, when team owners formed CART. They had seen, in the changing of the guard after Hulman's death and the USAC plane crash, an opportunity to challenge the status quo.

But this time it was young Mr. George who seized the moment.

With the exception of the hastily staged Harvest Classic in 1916, the annual "500" had been the only race at the Speedway since 1911. Tony thought devoting some of the down time to another great race seemed like a good use of the facility. Enter NASCAR with tire tests in 1992 and '93 and the first Brickyard 400 in 1994.

Furthermore, revenue from a second race could help finance a magnificent multi-million dollar facility makeover, which would pave the way for still another great race. Enter Formula One in 2000.

The break with tradition incensed "500" purists, but the logic seemed sound. Three sell-out races a year not only did more for the bottom line than one, they elevated the Speedway to the front rank on two more auto racing fronts.

Meanwhile, the tension surrounding the "500" was palpable.

Off the track, management upheaval, governance matters, and conflict between the haves and the have-nots had CART in about the same wounded state USAC had been 10 years earlier. Since he was the only CART member with a large stake in the company supplying engines to his teams and those of his competitors, Roger Penske caught his share of the flak.

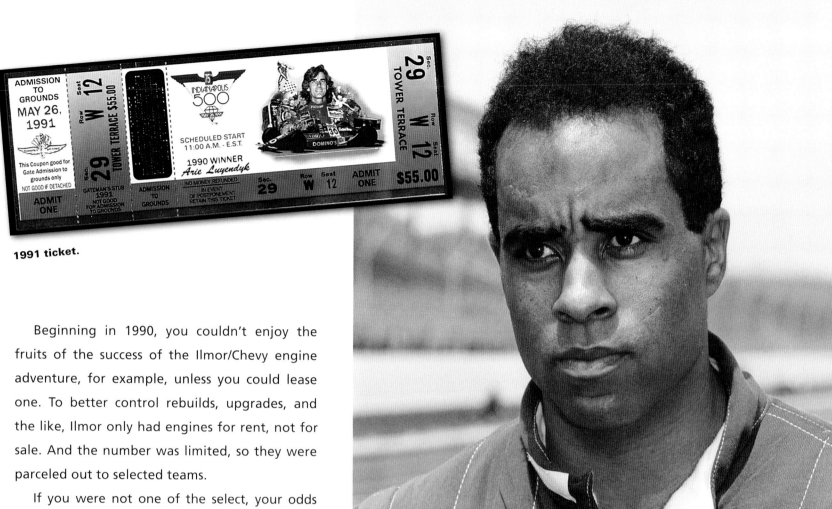

1991 ticket.

Beginning in 1990, you couldn't enjoy the fruits of the success of the Ilmor/Chevy engine adventure, for example, unless you could lease one. To better control rebuilds, upgrades, and the like, Ilmor only had engines for rent, not for sale. And the number was limited, so they were parceled out to selected teams.

If you were not one of the select, your odds were long, indeed, at the "500." As those infamous Chevrolet billboards proudly trumpeted, you couldn't win without one. Six teams fielded 10 Chevy-powered cars in the 1990 race. Chevys were one through six at the end.

At least one spectator took note. The banner he carried featured the CART logo and the words: Chevy And Rich Team owners.

On the track, railbirds had declared time and again over the years that the four-wheeled missiles of the "500" had reached terminal velocity. They said it when Barney Oldfield broke the 100-mph barrier in 1916. They said it again in 1989, when Mears topped 224. Just since 1980, pole speeds had surged by 30 miles an hour.

In 1991, road racing veteran Willy T. Ribbs was the first black driver to make the "500."

"INDY MOTOR SPEEDWAY OWNERS AND CEOS"

The Indianapolis 500's flavor and traditions have endured in part because of the ownership stability of the Indianapolis Motor Speedway. Only twice has the property changed hands. The Carl Fisher partnership sold it to Eddie Rickenbacker's group in 1927. Tony Hulman bought it in 1945.

Carl Fisher in the early 1900s.

Eddie Rickenbacker, circa 1920.

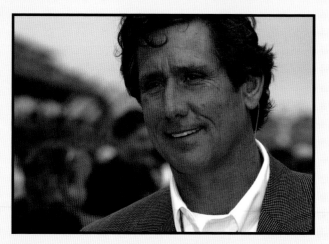

Speedway CEO Tony George in 2004.

(L to R) Tony Hulman, Wilbur Shaw and Theodore "Pop" Myers in 1945.

Long-time IMS executive Jeff Belskus assumed presidency on July 1, 2009. *IMS Photo by Ron McQueeney.*

To set the stage, it's 1991. Michael Andretti (No. 10) had done the unthinkable in Turn 1 on Lap 187 by passing Rick Mears (No. 3) on the outside for the lead. This is the scene one lap later. They're running about 220 mph, and Mears returns the favor. Mears goes on to win the race.

Lyn St. James' 11th-place finish earned her Rookie-of-the-Year honors in 1992.

Tony George

Tony Hulman's grandson Tony George promised change when he picked up the reins at the Speedway in 1990. He delivered with the formation of the Indy Racing League, a sweeping decade-long makeover of the Speedway's physical plant, the addition of the Brickyard 400 race in 1994, Formula One (from 2000 to 2007) and the Moto GP motorcycle race in 2008. He stepped down as track CEO after the 2009 "500."

Veteran Emerson Fittipaldi stretched the envelope a little with a pole speed of 225.30 in 1990. Arie Luyendyk won the race at a record speed of 185.981 mph, fully 15 mph faster than it had ever been run before.

Rick Mears, whose crash during practice was his first in 14 years of Indy racing, captured the pole for an unprecedented sixth time in 1991. He and Michael Andretti brought a crowd of 350,000 to its feet in the waning moments of the race. They were dueling for the lead when they each passed the other on the *outside* in Turn 1 on successive laps. When it was over, Mears was a four-time Indy winner. It was Penske's ninth as a car owner.

Not long after the 1991 race, an effort to provide low-budget teams typically running only at Indy with a less-expensive but competitive engine choice led to an adjustment in USAC rules. A requirement that push-rod engines be production-based was eliminated. Displacement could still be 3.8 liters, and turbochargers could run at 55 pounds boost, 10 more than their smaller, race-bred cousins.

1991 Dodge Viper pace car driven by Carroll Shelby.

Three years later, Penske's total domination of the 1994 race with just such an engine created a brouhaha that made the Ilmor/Chevy contretemps seem like a pillow fight.

But meanwhile, more room had to be made on the speed chart. Jim Crawford's unofficial 233.433 mph lap during practice in 1992 laid waste to the 230 barrier. Race day was cold, windy, and replete with crashes. At the end, Al Unser Jr. was ahead by just half a car length (.043 second) over Scott Goodyear. It was the closest finish in "500" history.

1990 program.

Although he sustains a head injury that ends his "500" racing career, Stan Fox breaks no bones in this spectacular crash in the first turn of the first lap of the 1995 race. Paul Tracy (No. 3 car behind #25) barely avoids a collision, but Eddie Cheever is not so lucky. Experts later determine that Cheever's contact with the Fox car probably lessened Stan's injuries.

1991 program.

Longtime Indianapolis 500 Chief Steward Tom Binford.

Some of the giants hung up their driving gloves in the next couple of years.

Rick Mears and A.J. Foyt both made surprise announcements: Rick at a Penske Racing Christmas party in 1992, A.J. after exiting his car on Pole Day in '93. As practice commenced in 1994, Al Unser and Johnny Rutherford joined them. All together, the four had graced indy's winner's circle 15 times.

The seeds USAC planted three years earlier with a small change to the language of an engine rule bore fruit for Roger Penske in 1994. Drawn by Ilmor's Mario Illien and developed and tested in total secrecy, the new V8 had the requisite two-valve push-rod architecture. Otherwise, it was a purpose-built race engine. Nobody would fess up regarding horsepower, but given its displacement and allotted turbo boost, 1,000 hp seemed a conservative estimate. That was a good 200 hp more than a Cosworth in qualifying trim.

The new Ilmor was badged a Mercedes, but it almost certainly would have been a Chevy had

1999 Chevy Monte Carlo pace car driven by Jay Leno.

a handshake agreement in late 1992 between Penske and Chevrolet General Manager Jim Perkins stayed in effect. The agreement would have extended GM's one-fourth ownership stake in Ilmor. It came apart when Chevy opted not to counter an offer Penske later received from the German company.

The engine's existence was revealed in a news conference a month before Opening Day. The outcry was immediate, but directed more toward rule-makers.

Even as Fittipaldi, Al Unser Jr., and Paul Tracy piloted the three Penske cars to the top of the speed charts during practice, there were howls about sandbagging.

As predicted, two Penskes were on the front row, and they dominated the race. Fittipaldi was close to becoming the first back-to-back "500" winner since Al's dad in 1971 with just 15 laps to go when he went low in Turn 4, got into the rumble strip now defining the inside edge of the track, lost control, and rode into the wall. Al Jr., who was in second place almost a full lap behind at the time, brought home the win.

USAC rewrote the rules before the 1995 race to lower the turbo boost, and the Mercedes mystery engine raced no more.

Ironically, without all that power available to overcome severe chassis deficiencies, none of the three cars making up Penske's team were able to qualify for the 1995 race. Jacques Villeneuve came from two laps down to win after Scott Goodyear was black-flagged for passing the pace car on Lap 190.

1998 program.

1992 ticket.

1992 tower suite ticket.

"LOW TECH / HIGH TECH "

In 100 years, the machinery and methods of operation at the Indianapolis 500 have run the gamut from blacksmith tech to the space age.

Early fueling a can at a time.

1980s pit stop choreography.

In the beginning, megaphonic amplification.

IMS press room scene, 21st Century.

Clean goggles? Jim Rathmann just needs to ask in 1955.

Graham Rahal's 2009 helmet is a work of art.

RPM SHIFT LIGHTS: LEDs illuminate and change color in sync with engine speed.

PI DASH: Informs a driver about the lap times, oil, water and gearbox temperatures and fuel mileage.

TALK BUTTON: Activates a microphone in the drivers's helmet.

PIT LANE SPEED LIMITER: Activates the engine control program, which limits a car's speed on pit lane.

RESET: During a pitstop, a driver pushes this button to reset the fuel reading on his display.

WEIGHT JACKER: Allows a driver to ajust the car's cross-weight in the course of the race.

FUEL MAP SWITCH: Allows a driver to adjust the engine's air/fuel mixture to increase mileage or to increase power.

PUSH-TO-PASS BUTTON: Sets fuel map at 100% rich for exra power to compete a pass or hold off another car.

DASH SCROLL BUTTON: Lets the driver select information to be displayed on PI dash.

FUEL/ALARM RESET

RADIO ↑ LIMITER ↓

← WJ → OT

NEUT

ARB MAP FUEL USED SPEED WJ DMP
MPG
FUEL TANK

FAULT

FUEL MAP

A

B

←PAGE→

One hundred years ago, an Indy car's huge steering wheel was just that and the dashboard contained a tachometer and little else. Today, the "dashboard" is virtually non-existent and the tiny steering wheel contains upwards of a dozen displays, switches, and buttons.

Eddie Cheever, who cut his teeth in international road racing, ran strong all day on his way to Victory Circle in 1998.

But Tony George, now just five years into his Speedway presidency and with the inaugural Brickyard 400 NASCAR race under his belt, made the biggest news. He announced that as of 1996, the "500" would be contested under the

1990 ticket.

Flawless pit stops and excellent tire management on a day when other front-runners suffer excessive tire wear reward Arie Luyendyk with victory in 1990.

auspices of the newly formed Indy Racing League. Furthermore, the IRL would sanction a new series in direct competition with CART.

The idea was to provide a lower-cost oval-track racing alternative that would reverse

With the start of the 1995 race just a few seconds away, cars bunch in Turn 1 on the pace lap.

the trend toward street circuits, and attract more talent from America's open-wheel minor leagues. Although IRL rules called for phasing in less expensive chassis and non-turbo engines, there would be a transition year. What ran at the "500" in 1995 would be legal in '96. Railbirds held their hats.

Amid an escalating war of words, the stage was set in 1996 for the fastest May in "500" history. With 25 of 33 starting spots guaranteed to IRL teams, CART regulars opted not to submit entries. That left "500" veterans such as Luyendyk, Robert Guerrero, Eddie Cheever, Scott Brayton, Buddy Lazier, John Paul Jr., and Lyn St. James to mix it up with rookies like Tony Stewart and Buzz Calkins, who won the IRL's inaugural race at Walt Disney World Speedway.

Stewart set the bar with a 237.336 practice lap. Luyendyk raised it with an unbelievable 239.260. That's less than an eye-wink shy of 240—three times faster than Indy's earliest-day warriors could make the circuit.

Pole Day saw Scott Brayton qualifying fastest with an official four-lap run of 233.718. When Luyendyk's attempt was disallowed (his car was underweight), he came back the next day to post what will likely stand as the all-time fastest official lap ever turned at the Speedway: 237.498.

Then, tragedy struck. Brayton was fatally injured when he crashed while testing race day setups in a back-up car. A somber Tony Stewart was moved into Brayton's number-one starting spot, and he brought the field to the green flag.

1999 program.

When the day was done, it was Buddy Lazier in Victory Circle.

With everybody in cars powered by thundering 4-liter production-based engines, 1997 made up in raucous noise what it lost in speed. Luyendyk captured the pole at a tick over 218 mph and went on to win his second "500." Scott Goodyear was a half-second behind at the checkered flag.

Through the remainder of the decade and on into the 21st Century, pole speeds hovered in the mid-220s.

That's 1985 Indy champ Danny Sullivan in the VISA car racing with Andre Ribeiro in 1995.

After two days of rain, the 81st Indianapolis 500 is about to resume in 1997. Since Tony Stewart was ahead when the race was halted on Day 2, he leads the field out of the pit area on Day 3.

It's a tradition of sorts that all crew members have a hand on their car as they move it from the garage area to the track on race day. Marco Greco's No. 16 started and finished 14th in 1998.

Pit crews spend endless hours rehearsing, as even a fraction of a second delay can cost a driver a position or even the race.

Kenny Brack takes on fuel and new tires on his way to victory in 1999.

Finessing his way to a surprise victory in 2006, Sam Hornish Jr. leaves his pit in a cloud of tire smoke. The white-haired gentleman standing high to the left is car owner Roger Penske.

THE ROARING 2000s
2000-2010

" *I've traveled all over the world, and every place I go, the one thing everyone wants to talk about is Indy, Indy, Indy. What I tell 'em is, yeah, you got it right—there just isn't anything in the world like the Indianapolis 500.* **"**

A.J. Foyt

As dawn broke on the new millenium, the signs were there for all to see that the Indianapolis 500 was entering a new era. The stage had undergone a giant makeover, and big-name players who had been gone awhile were returning.

Tens of millions of dollars had been invested in site enhancements to accommodate the Brickyard

Chip Ganassi

Chip Ganassi started five Indys as a driver. He became a part owner of Patrick Racing in 1989, when Emerson Fittipaldi gave the team a "500" win. He started his own team in 1990. Absent from the "500" as CART and the IRL went separate ways in the late '90s, Target Chip Ganassi was the first front-line CART team to return in 2000. It was promptly rewarded with Juan Pablo Montoya's "500" win.

400 and the Formula One United States Grand Prix, which was coming in September.

Now more than 90 years old, the track never looked or worked better. And Tony George's 1990s vision of three great races a year was about to be realized.

What's more, CART superpower Chip Ganassi had purchased two IndyCar Series cars for drivers Juan Pablo Montoya and Jimmy Vasser. Ganassi hadn't raced at Indianapolis since the advent of the rival Indy Racing League in 1995. Sponsor considerations and the lure of Indy's riches and prestige brought him back.

When Montoya, an international road racing star but a rookie at Indianapolis, won the 2000 race and Vasser finished seventh, $1.44 million of the $9.5 million purse disbursed at the Victory Dinner went to Ganassi's team.

In 2001, more CART teams found themselves under pressure from their sponsors to participate in the "500." The race winner, plus the five cars immediately behind him, were all CART regulars.

Roger Penske's cars, driven by Helio Castroneves and Gil de Ferran, finished one-two. Michael Andretti was third, followed by three Ganassi cars.

Castroneves won again in 2002. Paul Tracy had gone around him with a lap to go, but because the caution lights flashed for an incident elsewhere on the track before the Tracy pass was complete, it was disallowed.

By 2003, CART's strongest teams had made the switch to the Indy Racing League. The Penske, Ganassi, Mo Nunn, and Barry Green organizations were among the first.

A work of art in pre-dawn light, the Speedway's 10-story Pagoda control tower pays subtle homage to the Japanese-style structure that first served the purpose in the early teens.

Comedian David Letterman, an Indianapolis native, partnered with Bobby Rahal to form a new IRL team.

In 2002, with GM's Oldsmobile Division shutting down, the Aurora V8 that had powered the bulk of the Indy field since 1997 was replaced by a smaller, lighter Chevrolet engine.

Both Toyota and Honda entered the fray in 2003, with Honda emerging in 2006 as the sole IndyCar Series engine supplier. Honda's partner on the Indy project was Ilmor Engineering of England, the company that produced the Chevy Indy engines of the 1980s and early '90s and the Mercedes engine of 1994.

A MODERN INDY 500 ENGINE

Ten features that set this engine apart from a typical production V8.

1 These carbon fiber intake horns route air from the mouth in the bodywork above the driver's head directly into each cylinder.

2 Large aircraft-quality fuel lines and rails appear oversize, but they must accommodate a flood of ethanol. Indy cars drink about a gallon per lap.

3 When torqued tightly to the bulkhead at these attachment points, the engine becomes an integral chassis element.

4 Pent-roof combustion chambers are designed around the four valves per cylinder that open and close almost 200 times a second.

5 An elegant system of lightweight steel gears manages the rotation of the four camshafts.

Illustration courtesy of David Kimble.

6 There's one high-pressure fuel injector per intake valve.

7 A low-inertia flat-plane crankshaft eliminates counterweights and permits quicker acceleration. Overlapping firing pulses produce a signature high-pitched exhaust sound.

8 An ignition coil is mounted atop each spark plug, which fires from a position in the roof of the combustion chamber.

9 Precisely sized and curved headers feed exhaust gasses into a massive tail pipe.

10 A gear-driven modular dry sump lubrication system eliminates a bulky oil pan and allows for lower engine placement in the car.

David Kimble

Eventual winner Dan Wheldon (No. 26) and 1999 "500" champ Kenny Brack are side by side on a restart in 2005.

Indy 500 winner Eddie Cheever was a car owner in 2005, and these are both his entries. That's Alex Barron in No. 51, Patrick Carpentier in No. 83.

From the IndyCar Series' inception, more teams used the Italian-built Dallara chassis than anything else. But when Penske driver Gil de Ferran outran teammate Castroneves to win the 2003 race, he was wheeling a new Panoz G Force.

The win was Penske's 13th and the third in a row. In the history of the "500," only one other car owner had scored the hat trick, Lou Moore of the late 1940s Blue Crown dynasty.

As speeds crept back into the 230 mph range, IndyCar Series officals imposed an engine displacement reduction in 2004 from 3.5 to 3 liters. It had the desired effect. Rahal Letterman Racing driver Buddy Rice was pole position qualifier at 222.024 mph, nine miles an hour slower than the previous year. Rain halted the race on Lap 180 with Rice in the lead. His share of the $10.3 million distributed at the Victory Dinner was almost $1.8 million.

When 19-year-old Danica Patrick visited the paddock at an IndyCar Series in Kentucky in 2001, not that many people paid heed. The tiny teenager from Roscoe, Illinois, had been successfully competing on the European Formula Ford circuit, but she was a virtual unknown in the U.S.

It was a different story in 2005, however, when Patrick took Indianapolis by storm. Driving for Rahal Letterman Racing, she almost won the pole. She led three times, the last after a daring move inside British driver Dan Wheldon on a restart with 10 laps to go. She finished fourth, which made her Rookie-of-the-Year selection a foregone conclusion.

Wheldon won the race for Andretti Green Racing. But Patrick won the attention of millions of race fans. And the macho world of motor racing had a new poster girl.

Forty Indys after he won the 1967 pole, the Speedway masses saluted Mario Andretti, his son

Helio Castroneves

Helio Castroneves of Brazil won the "500" in 2001, 2002, and 2009, making him one of only nine three-time winners. Castoneves is known as "Spiderman" for climbing the debris fence to celebrate his victories.

A 1935 rehab removed high banks in corners and altered outer walls to keep drivers taking a high line from being launched over the walls.

Rudi Caracciola was badly hurt in this car in 1946. Tank-like structure left early Indy cars intact but transferred high energy loads to occupants.

Sam Hornish's broken car comes in on the hook after a Lap 104 crash that also took out Darren Manning and Greg Ray in 2004. Modern race cars are designed to absorb energy by breaking up on impact.

"SAFETY: AN ONGOING ENDEAVOR"

Until the late 1990s, hard walls around racetracks were considered the price racers paid to protect spectators. The notion of a softer wall first took the form of a system at Indianapolis called the PEDS Barrier, consisting of overlapping composite plates, which was succeeded in 2002 by the award-winning SAFER (Steel and Foam Energy Reduction) Barrier. Since then, SAFER Barriers have been incorporated into every IndyCar and NASCAR track. Taken together, more forgiving walls and race cars designed to dissipate impact energy may be the most significant safety enhancement in the history of the Speedway.

SAFER Barrier under construction.

The PEDS Barrier with overlapping plates lasted several years, and contributed to development of the SAFER Barrier.

As designed, Jeff Bucknum's car No. 44 sheds appendages and energy in a 2005 encounter with the SAFER Barrier.

1

2

3

4

The Speedway's celebrated SAFER Barrier has made contact with Indy's unforgiving walls a lot less hazardous. But other major safety features helped Mike Conway and others survive a horrendous crash two laps from the end of the 2010 "500." Conway's car was running about 220 mph when it touched wheels with Ryan Hunter-Reay's slower-moving machine, which was low on fuel. A split second later, Hunter-Reay is sliding along the SAFER Barrier and Conway is airborne and into a cable-reinforced catch fence (Photo 1 and 2), which redirects his car back toward the racing surface. Another split second and Hunter-Reay slips beneath Conway's disintegrating car (Photo 3). The carbon-fiber "tub" in which Conway is cocooned lands on the track as cars whiz by (Photos 4 and 5).

Because the cables held, the car dissipated energy as it broke up, and the tub remained intact, Conway escaped with a broken leg and back injuries. He will race again.

5

Roger Penske

Roger Penske is the winningest car owner in Indianapolis history and one of the most repected figures on the global racing stage. Already a veteran of the Trans-Am and Can-Am wars of the late '60s, he won the "500" for the first time with Mark Donohue in 1972. Helio Castroneves gave him number 15 in 2009.

Michael, and 19-year-old grandson Marco before the start of the 2006 race.

And what a race it would be for the last few laps. Sam Hornish Jr., who was well off the pace and a good half-lap down with less than 20 to go, won it by .0635 of a second over Marco, who had seized the lead on Lap 197 from his father, who had taken it just three laps earlier from Tony Kanaan. Three hundred thousand people at the track, and millions more tuned to radios and TVs around the world, gasped in unison.

The strategy that put Hornish in position to win was classic Roger Penske. First, he brought Hornish in for fuel at the last possible moment before a restart with 39 laps left. Then, he had the youngster from Defiance, Ohio, ease up to where he was losing almost a second a lap to the leaders. With 10 to go, the front-runners pitted for fuel. Hornish stayed out, regained speed, and suddenly, out of nowhere, was...there.

The winner's share of the $10,518,000 purse was $1,745,000.

2000 Oldsmobile Aurora pace car driven by Anthony Edwards.

2002 program.

2000 ticket.

Scott Sharp (No. 8) leads a formation through Turn 1 early in the 2006 race. Sharp started 8th, finished 9th.

Grandson A.J. Foyt IV and his grandfather share a moment before the 2003 "500."

The rolling artwork that Jeff Ward is driving in 2001 is getting serviced during a pit stop. He starts 8th, finishes 24th.

Dario Franchitti won the rain-shortened 2007 race.

A couple of really big things happened on the way to the 2008 "500."

The Speedway announced in October that the purse, which had hovered in the $10.5 million range, would soar by at least 25 percent for 2008 to $13.4 million. (Actually, it topped $14 million by race time.)

And on February 22, 2008, Tony George and owners of Champ Car, which had acquired the assets of CART in bankruptcy court, signed a historic agreement effectively ending the 30-year conflict over the governance of big-league open wheel racing in America.

Scott Dixon won the 2008 race for Chip Ganassi's Target team by slightly more than a second over Panther Racing's Vitor Meira. His share of the purse was almost $2.99 million.

The 2009 "500" began a three-year Centennial Era celebration at the Speedway.

On Pole Day, Castroneves qualified a tad slower than Penske teammate Ryan Briscoe, then returned

2006 program.

2001 Oldsmobile Bravada driven by Elaine Irwin-Mellencamp.

2009 program.

International racing star Jackie Stewart, who was Rookie of the Year at the "500" in 1966, came back in 2005 for a Race Day visit.

Race team owner and Indianapolis native David Letterman in 2003.

to the track later for a second attempt. This time, his 224.864 mph four-lap run put him on the pole. The race saw Castroneves lead 66 laps on his way to his third "500" win. It was Penske's 15th. The team's share of the $14.3 million purse was a little over $3 million.

Several weeks later, Tony George, whose imprint was everywhere on almost 20 years of Speedway and "500" history, stepped down as CEO. Six months later, he resigned his seat on the board of directors of Hulman & Company, the family entity that owns the track and the Indy Racing League.

As the dust settled, after long-time Speedway executive and new President and CEO Jeff Belskus vigorously denied the track might be for sale, Speedway history buffs likened the episode to crisis moments of the past. They were numerous.

A poster-quality view of pit action during the 2003 race. The vastness of the setting and the way the light plays on tire marks left by cars accelerating back into racing makes this a particularly interesting study.

Scott Dixon (No. 9) narrowly misses Dan Wheldon (No. 26), who gets airborne on Lap 186 in the 2003 race.

2003 ticket.

NORTHEAST VISTA $75.00 Sec 37 Row MM Seat 7

Helio Castroneves • 2001 - 2002 Indy 500 Champion

NORTHEAST VISTA $75.00 Sec 37 Row MM Seat 7

ADMIT ONE

Sun. May 25, 2003

NOT GOOD IF DETACHED

Thirty-three race team spotters, one policeman, and ABC-TV people have the roof of a Turn 1 grandstand to themselves during the 2003 race.

Upset about hotel rate gouging, Carl Fisher once raged that he would move the "500" to Cincinnati.

He had to be talked out of selling the track in 1923, after a wave of post World War I patriotism resulted in a bill banning "commercial sports" on Memorial Day passed the Indiana General Assembly.

Eddie Rickenbacker mothballed the property during WW II.

The post-war ASPAR driver's union flap nearly dealt the race a killer blow.

Tony Hulman's death and the formation of CART clouded its future in the late 1970s.

The founding of the IRL in the mid-'90s was an end-game maneuver intended to unify big-league open-wheel racing around the "500" or die trying.

Sam Hornish Jr. leads early in the 2006 race. A pit stop miscue seemed to ruin his chances, but he stormed from half a lap down with 20 laps remaining to win by less than a tenth of a second over rookie Marco Andretti.

Sarah Fisher drove for Dreyer & Reinbold Racing in 2007. She started 21st, finished 18th.

Mari Hulman George, (left) chairman of the board of the Indianapolis Motor Speedway, with television personality and Indiana native Florence Henderson before the start of the 2007 "500."

Danica Patrick (No. 7) crosses the yard of bricks a few feet ahead of Marco Andretti (No. 26) and moves into second place following a rain delay midway in the 2007 race. Marco crashed after tangling with Dan Wheldon late in the race. He was scored 24th. When another storm halted the race at Lap 166, Danica was 8th.

Helio Castroneves with girlfriend Adriana Henao before the start of the 2010 race.

The eyes have it in 2008, as a camera catches Danica Patrick in a pre-race moment.

As race fans looked forward to 2011 and the 100th anniversary of the first "500," it seemed presumptuous in the extreme to distill the phenomenon into a sound bite.

But if two little words could encapsulate all the thrills and spills, the emotion, the triumphs and tragedies, the drama, the politics and pageantry of the Indianapolis 500, they might well be…. *Greatness endures.*

What seemed like total chaos was actually a very finely choreographed dance as a late-race caution brought the field into the pits in 2008. That's Dario Franchitti in the red car exiting just ahead of Tony Kanaan.

Brian Barnhart, president, competition and operations division, Indy Racing League, gives last-minute directions to Hideki Mutoh before his qualifying run in 2008. Mutoh started 9th, finished 7th.

An ethanol fire during a pit stop delays Vitor Meira's return to action in 2009.

A.J. Foyt with driver Vitor Meira before the start of the 2009 race.

Graham Rahal, who started fourth in 2009, walks Indy's sacred ground with dad Bobby, who won the 1986 race.

Celebrating his 15th Indianapolis 500 win, Roger Penske shakes hands with Tim Cindric, president of Penske's racing division and manager of Helio Castroneves' 2009 team.

Two of the best known symbols of the Indianapolis 500: The long-tailed Marmon Wasp, winner of the first "500," and the sterling silver Borg-Warner Trophy.

2005 ticket.

The 2007 field stretches out behind Helio Castroneves.

Forced high in a turn as he leads the "500" in 2008, Tony Kanaan spins and is collected by Sarah Fisher.

The No. 23 car of Milka Duno makes contact with the SAFER Barrier in 2007.

Television personality Robin Roberts prepares to drive the Chevy Camaro 2010 pace car.

Joie Chitwood III is at the wheel of the 2002 Corvette pace car.

Movie star Jack Nicholson wields the green flag to start the 2010 race.

Entertainer Ashley Judd watches her husband, Dario Franchitti, in the 2010 race.

Dario Franchitti becomes a two-time Indianapolis 500 winner in 2010. He won his first "500" in 2007.

Along with long-time friend and counselor Jack Snyder, Mari Hulman George and her daughters constitute the board of directors of the Indianapolis Motor Speedway. Left to right are daughters Kathi, Nancy and Josie, Mr. Snyder, Mari, and son Tony, who relinquished his seat on the board in early 2010.

Ray Harroun's 1911 Marmon

...was one of the first race cars acquired for the Hall of Fame Museum. The Marmon Wasp (first nicknamed the "yellow jacket" because of its long pointed tail) has been restored to running condition. It is occasionally driven in Speedway ceremonies.

Joe Dawson, Winner 1912 "National"

Joe Dawson's 1912 National

...is part of the Hall of Fame Museum collection.

WHERE ARE THEY NOW?

The Fate of the Winning Cars

No question when Tony Hulman's friend Karl Kizer started rounding up relics for the Hall of Fame Museum in the early '50s, interest in old "500" machinery perked up. Until then, yesterday's race cars had a lot in common with yesterday's newspapers.

More than a half-century later, provenance issues still make a roster of Indianapolis 500 winners a work in progress. After asking "Where are they now?" the next question might well be: "How do you know?" We offer these with due respect to differing viewpoints.

Jules Goux's 1913 Peugeot

...was actually built in 1912 for Grand Prix racing in Europe. Sold off when Peugeot disbanded its racing operation in 1915, its whereabouts are unknown.

Rene Thomas' 1914 Delage

...is part of the Hall of Fame Museum collection. Thomas was 88 years old in 1973, when he was driven around the track in the riding mechanic's seat as a highlight of pre-race ceremonies.

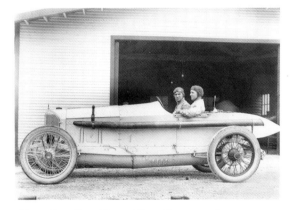

Ralph DePalma's 1915 Mercedes

...had been a factory entry in the 1914 French Grand Prix. Sold to a Chicago sportsman, the car was in Germany when hostilities leading up to World War I broke out. The car and DePalma barely made it out of the country. Its current whereabouts are unknown.

WHERE ARE THEY NOW?

Dario Resta's 1916 Peugeot

...was actually a 1913 Grand Prix car. A car with significant documentation and said to be the '16 winner made a Speedway appearance on race day in 1966. It's believed to be in a California collection.

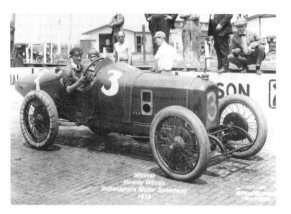

Howdy Wilcox's 1919 Peugeot

...was another of the factory cars of the early teens. It was one of two Peugeots prepared in Jim Allison's Speedway shop for Wilcox and Jules Goux, who finished third. It is unlikely the car still exists.

Gaston Chevrolet's 1920 Monroe

...apparently was not rebuilt after it was destroyed in the crash that took Gaston's life six months after the "500."

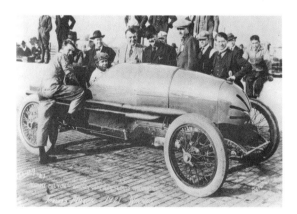

Tommy Milton's 1921 Frontenac

...another of the Chevrolet brothers' innovative race cars, its whereabouts are unknown.

Jimmy Murphy's 1922 Duesenberg Murphy Special

...also won the 1921 French Grand Prix. Now a part of the Speedway's Hall of Fame museum collection, it has been restored to running condition.

Tommy Milton's 1923 Miller

...was the first 100 percent pure Miller to win Indianapolis. Its whereabouts are unconfirmed.

The L.L. Corum/ Joe Boyer 1924 Duesenberg

...was one of several '24 Duesies fitted with centrifugal superchargers. Corum drove the first half of the race, then relinquished to Boyer. Its whereabouts are unconfirmed.

Peter DePaolo's 1925 Duesenberg

...is also believed to be the 1927 Indy 500 winner (with George Souders at the wheel). Its whereabouts are unknown.

Frank Lockhart's 1926 Miller

...was a new rear-drive machine commissioned by sportsman driver Peter Kreis, who came down with pneumonia just before the race. Lockhart was tapped to replace him. The rookie sensation had a two-lap lead over the second-place car when rain halted the race at the 400-mile mark. The car's whereabouts are unknown.

Louis Meyer's 1928 Miller

...Owned now by the Hall of Fame Museum, it has been restored to running condition. Meyer drove it during race day ceremonies in 1978 and again in 1986, which was the 50th anniversary of his third Indy 500 victory.

Ray Keech's 1929 Simplex

...Its current whereabouts are unconfirmed.

Billy Arnold's 1930 Miller-Hartz

...was a new naturally aspirated front-drive two-man Miller that Arnold qualified on the pole and led 198 of the 200 laps. It was the first car to run the "500" at average speed of over 100 mph. Its current whereabouts are unknown.

WHERE ARE THEY NOW?

Louis Schneider's 1931 Bowes Seal Fast Miller

...participated in the Speedway's vintage car show and parade in 2003 and was displayed at the Amelia Island Concours d' Elegance in 2004. It is privately owned.

Fred Frame's 1932 Miller-Hartz

...was originally entered for Billy Durant's son Cliff. Rebodied, it is now restored to running condition and is part of the Hall of Fame Museum collection.

Louis Meyer's 1933 Tydol Miller

...is said to be in a private collection.

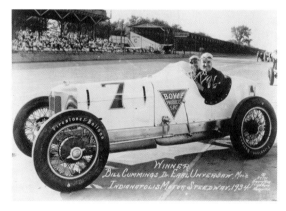

Bill Cummings' 1934 Boyle Miller

...is believed to be in a private collection in Indiana.

Kelly Petillo's 1935 Gilmore Speedway Special

...is believed to have been destroyed and never rebuilt.

Louis Meyer's 1936 Ring Free Miller

...is said to be in a private collection.

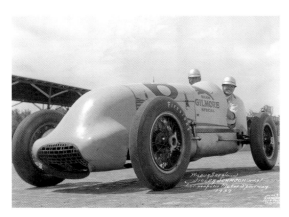

Wilbur Shaw's 1937 Shaw-Gilmore Special

...had been driven by Shaw in the '36 race. It was also driven by Mauri Rose (1939), Billy DeVore (1940) and Frank Wearne ('41 and '46). It was the car Paul Russo drove in '47 and Joie Chitwood in '48. It was demolished in a crash at the Speedway in 1949 and is believed never rebuilt.

Floyd Roberts' 1938 Burd Piston Ring Special

...is the car Roberts was driving in '39 when he perished in a crash. Rebuilt and raced in 1940, it was unsalvageable after a wreck in Atlanta in 1946 that took George Robson's life.

Wilbur Shaw's 1939/40 Boyle Special Maserati

...is restored to running condition at the Hall of Fame Museum. Wilbur's son Bill and grandson Peter have both driven it during Speedway events.

The Floyd Davis/ Mauri Rose 1941 Noc-Out Hose Clamp Special

...is believed to have been driven in six 500s as well as an open-wheel race series NASCAR sanctioned in 1952, where Buck Baker drove it to the championship. The car has been restored and is part of the Hall of Fame Museum collection.

George Robson's 1946 Thorne Engineering Special

...was driven in five post-war Indy 500s and four pre-war races. Now part of the Hall of Fame collection, it has been restored to running condition. It was driven in 1985 pre-race ceremonies by Tony George to commemorate the 40th anniversary of the family's ownership of the track.

Mauri Rose's 1947/48 Blue Crown Spark Plug Special

...was donated to the Hall of Fame Museum. Restored to running condition, it was driven by Johnny Rutherford during pre-race ceremonies in 2002.

WHERE ARE THEY NOW?

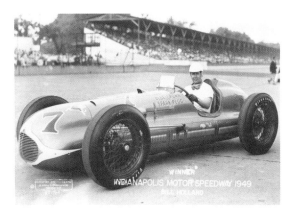

Bill Holland's 1949 Blue Crown Spark Plug Special

...is believed in a private collection in Michigan. On display for many years at the Museum of Science and Industry in Chicago, it was in running condition in 1996, when it appeared at the Goodwood Festival of Speed in England.

Johnnie Parsons' 1950 Wynn's Friction Proofing Special

...is the car Parsons raced in three Indys and to the AAA national championship in 1949. Parsons drove it on race morning in 1980. It is part of the Hall of Fame Museum collection.

Lee Wallard's 1951 Belanger Special

...is part of the Hall of Fame collection. Restored to running condition, it has been driven on numerous ceremonial occasions by Gary Bettenhausen. Mauri Rose Jr. drove it during opening day ceremonies in 2003.

Troy Ruttman's 1952 Agajanian Special

...is in a California collection.

Bill Vukovich's 1953/54 Fuel Injection Special

...is the same car in which Vuky almost won the '52 race. Built by Frank Kurtis for oilman Howard Keck, it is considered the genesis car of the Speedway's roadster era. It is owned by the Hall of Fame Museum.

Bob Sweikert's 1955 John Zink Special

...is another Kurtis chassis. It has been restored and is owned by the Hall of Fame Museum. It apparently ran in only two Indys—the '55 and '56 races.

Pat Flaherty's 1956 John Zink Special

...is in possession of the Zink Museum near Tulsa. It was relocated to the Hall of Fame Museum for its 50th anniversary in 2006, where it was the centerpiece of a replica version of a mid-century Speedway garage.

Sam Hanks' 1957/ Jimmy Bryan's 1958 Belond Special

...is the car George Salih built in his California home and tried to sell but couldn't. Restored to running condition by the Hall of Fame Museum, it was driven by Hanks during ceremonies in 1982 commemorating the 25th anniversary of his victory.

Rodger Ward's 1959 Leader Card roadster

...was restored by A.J. Watson and is now in a private collection. It has appeared at the Pebble Beach Concours d' Elegance and at the Goodwood Festival of Speed.

Jim Rathmann's 1960 Ken Paul Special

...is the car in which Rathmann dueled with Rodger Ward in one of the most thrilling Indys ever. The lead changed over and over again in the last half of the race. The car is part of the Hall of Fame Museum collection. Rathmann has a replica in his Florida collection.

A.J. Foyt's 1961 Bowes Seal Fast Special

...is part of the Hall of Fame collection, which has restored it to running condition. Foyt has driven it a number of ceremonial laps at the track.

Rodger Ward's 1962 Leader Card Special

...was the car Don Branson drove in '63. Now a part of the Hall of Fame collection, it has been restored to running condition. Ward was at the wheel in 1982, when it made several ceremonial laps.

WHERE ARE THEY NOW?

Parnelli Jones' 1963 Agajanian Special

...nicknamed "Calhoun," it was driven in every 500 from 1960 through '64. In 1962, it was the first car to qualify at more than 150 mph. Owned by the Hall of Fame Museum, it has been restored to running condition. It was driven by Jones during the Parade of Champions celebration May 10, 1998.

A.J.Foyt's 1964 Sheraton-Thompson Special

...is likely the only Indy winner in existence that remains almost exactly as it was when it came off the track. It took part in the May 6, 2007, celebration where Foyt's winning cars were paraded.

Jim Clark's 1965 Lotus

...the first rear-engine (it's the four-cam Ford) car to win the "500," is owned and recently restored to running condition by the Henry Ford Museum in Dearborn, Michigan.

Graham Hill's 1966 American Red Ball Lola

...is one of three Lolas entered by Texan John Mecom. Returning in 1967, it was heavily damaged in a last-lap crash and is believed never rebuilt.

A.J. Foyt's 1967 Sheraton-Thompson Coyote

...is part of the Hall of Fame collection. On opening day in 2007, Larry Foyt drove it during festivities commemorating A.J.'s 50th year at the "500."

Bobby Unser's 1968 Rislone Special

...was also driven at the "500" in 1970 by Mike Mosley and in '71 by George Snider. It is owned by the Hall of Fame Museum.

Mario Andretti's 1969 STP Hawk

...was donated to the Smithsonian Institution in Washington, D.C. The Hall of Fame Museum has a replica.

Al Unser's 1970 Johnny Lightning Colt

...is part of a California collection.

Al Unser's 1971 Johnny Lightning Colt

...is part of a California collection.

Mark Donohue's 1972 Sunoco McLaren

...was donated to the Hall of Fame Museum, where it is usually on display. This is the only one of Roger Penske's 15 winning cars at the museum.

Gordon Johncock's 1973 STP Eagle

...is in a private collection in Michigan. The Hall of Fame Museum has a replica.

Johnny Rutherford's 1974 McLaren

...was on loan for many years at the Hall of Fame Museum. Now part of an Alabama collection, it was back at the Speedway in 2006, when Johnny Rutherford drove it during community day ceremonies.

WHERE ARE THEY NOW?

Bobby Unser's 1975 Jorgensen Eagle

... is now a part of a private collection in Florida.

Johnny Rutherford's 1976 Hy-Gain McLaren

...saw action in four Indianapolis 500s. Restored to display condition, it is now a part of a California collection.

A.J. Foyt's 1977 Gilmore Coyote

...is the property of the Hall of Fame Museum. A running restoration was driven during the 2007 A.J. Foyt 50th anniversary celebration by Foyt's grandson A.J. Foyt IV.

Al Unser's 1978 First National City Traveler's Checks Lola

...was restored and donated to the Hall of Fame Museum, where it is on normally on display.

Rick Mears' 1979 Gould Penske PC-6

...is the same car Mario Andretti drove in '78. Destroyed later in a crash, it was restored to running condition and is part of the Penske Racing Collection.

Johnny Rutherford's 1980 Chaparral

...which heralded the ground effects era at the "500" was restored and donated by Chaparral Racing Ltd. to the Hall of Fame Museum, where it is on permanent display.

Bobby Unser's 1981 Norton Penske PC-9B

...is currently in a California collection.

Gordon Johncock's 1982 STP Wildcat

...is part of the Hall of Fame Museum collection. It has been restored to running condition. Johncock drove it at the Speedway in 1998.

Tom Sneva's 1983 Texaco Star

...was donated to the Hall of Fame Museum. Restored to running condition, it was driven by Sneva during pre-race ceremonies in 1998.

Rick Mears' 1984 Pennzoil Z-7 March

...was restored to running condition and is part of the Penske Racing Collection.

Danny Sullivan's 1985 Miller High Life March

...was restored to running condition and is on display in the Penske Racing Collection.

Bobby Rahal's 1986 Budweiser/ Truesports March

...was restored by TrueSports after the '86 season and placed on display briefly at the Hall of Fame Museum. Now part of a private collection in Alabama, it has appeared at vintage racing and concours events.

WHERE ARE THEY NOW?

Al Unser's 1987 Cummins/Holset March 86C

...had been retired to show car status until it was commandeered for duty at the Indianapolis 500. It's the car (then Ilmor-powered) in which Rick Mears set a closed-course speed record August 1, 1986, and which Mears wheeled to a pole position start and a third-place finish at the "500" that year. Restored to running condition, it is part of the Penske Racing Collection.

Rick Mears' 1988 Pennzoil Z-7 PC-17

...is on display in the Penske Racing Collection, where it has been restored to running condition. It was on special display at the Hall of Fame Museum in 2008.

Emerson Fittipaldi's 1989 Marlboro Penske PC-18

...was a Penske customer car entered at the Indianapolis 500 by the Pat Patrick/Chip Ganassi team and then sold when the team was reorganized. Re-acquired for the Penske Racing Collection, it was restored to running condition. A replica is on display at a university in Brazil.

Arie Luyendyk's 1990 Domino's Pizza Lola

...winner of the fastest 500 ever, is a part of the Hall of Fame Museum collection. It has been restored to running condition.

Rick Mears' 1991 Marlboro Penske PC-20

...is the car in which Mears was injured during practice for the 1992 race. Restored to display condition, it is the property of the Penske Racing Collection.

Al Unser, Jr.'s 1992 Valvoline Galmer

...winner of the closest-ever "500," remains the possession of Ashland Oil Co., which brought it back to the track in 2002 for a re-creation of the finish-line scene.

Emerson Fittipaldi's 1993 Marlboro Penske PC-22

...has been restored to running condition and is on display in the Penske Racing Collection.

Al Unser, Jr.'s 1994 Marlboro Penske PC-23

...is one of three cars entered in '94 with Mercedes push-rod engines. Unser inherited the win after teammate Emerson Fittipaldi's late-race encounter with the wall. A part of the Penske Racing Collection, it was restored to running condition. It appeared at the Goodwood Festival of Speed in 2002.

Jacques Villeneuve's 1995 Player's Ltd Reynard

...is the property of the Hall of Fame museum.

Buddy Lazier's 1996 Delta Faucet Reynard

...was purchased by Hemelgarn Racing from the Chip Ganassi stable in late '95 and entered for Lazier in the first "500" under the auspices of the Indy Racing League. Still the possession of Hemelgarn, it has been displayed periodically at the Hall of Fame Museum.

Arie Luyendyk's 1997 Sprint/Miller Lite G-Force

...is the same car Luyendyk raced in the '98 "500." Sam Schmidt was driving it when he was severely injured in a crash at Texas Motor Speedway in 1999. Team owner Fred Treadway has restored it to display condition.

Eddie Cheever's 1998 Rachel's Potato Chips Dallara

...is in a private collection.

WHERE ARE THEY NOW?

Kenny Brack's 1999 Foyt Power Team Dallara

...is part of A.J. Foyt's collection. It was on display at the Hall of Fame Museum in 2007.

Juan Pablo Montoya's 2000 Target Chip Ganassi G-Force

...raced just once – the 2000 "500." Retired to the Ganassi collection, it was freshened for a pre-race parade lap in 2010.

Helio Castroneves' 2001 Marlboro Penske IRL 1

...is restored to running condition and is part of the Penske Racing Collection. Castroneves drove it during Speedway ceremonies in 2003 honoring back-to-back winners.

Helio Castroneves' 2002 Marlboro Penske IRL 2

...was retired to the Penske Racing Collection soon after the "500" win. It is in running condition.

Gil de Ferran's 2003 Marlboro Penske Panoz G Force

...is part of the Penske Racing Collection.

Buddy Rice's 2004 Rahal-Letterman Panoz

...was displayed on the White House lawn in July 2004, when the team went to meet the President. This is the car Rice crashed in practice for the '05 race. It was repaired and subsequently qualified by Kenny Brack. It is on display at the Honda Collection Hall in Motegi, Japan.

Dan Wheldon's 2005 Klein Tools/Jim Beam Dallara

...is still eligible for IRL duty.

Sam Hornish, Jr.'s 2006 Marlboro Team Penske Dallara

...is in running condition at the Penske Racing Collection along with a 2006 Corvette pace car replica.

Dario Franchitti's 2007 Canadian Club Dallara

...remains eligible for IRL competition. The car was heavily damaged when Franchitti crashed at Michigan International Raceway later in '07. It was rebuilt by Andretti Green Racing for driver Marco Andretti.

Scott Dixon's 2008 Target Chip Ganassi Dallara

...is one of three cars Dixon continues to drive in IRL competition.

Helio Castroneves' 2009 Team Penske Dallara

...was retired to the Penske Racing Collection but remains eligible for IRL competition.

Dario Franchitti's 2010 Target Chip Ganassi Dallara

...is one of three cars Franchitti continues to drive in IRL competition.

BIBLIOGRAPHY

Arnold, Dave. *Indy Race Cars, From Behind the Garage Door*. Osceola, WI: Motorbooks Intl.,1989.

Beck, Bill. *The Fastest Crowd Around*, 1999.

Binford, Tom. *A Checkered Past: My Twenty Years As Indy 500 Chief Steward*. Chicago: Cornerstone Press, 1993.

Bloemker, Al. *500 Miles To Go: The Story of the Indianapolis Motor Speedway*. London, England: Frederick Muller Ltd., 1961.

Borgeson, Griffith. *The Golden Age of the American Racing Car*. Warrendale, PA: SAE International, 1997.

Burns, John M. *Thunder at Sunrise: A History of the Vanderbilt Cup, the Grand Prize and the Indianapolis 500, 1904-1916*. Jefferson, NC: McFarland & Company, 2006.

Carnegie, Tom. *Indy 500, More than a Race*. New York: McGraw-Hill, 1986.

Davidson, Donald and Rick Shaffer. *Autocourse Official History of the Indianapolis 500*. Silverstone, England: Crash Media Group, Ltd, 2006.

Dees, Mark L. *The Miller Dynasty*. New York: Barnes Publishing Inc., 1981.

Foster, Mark S. *Castles in the Sand, the Life and Times of Carl Graham Fisher*. Gainesville, Florida: University Press of Florida, 2000.

Fox, Jack. *The Illustrated History of the 500*. Madison, IN: Carl Hungness Publishing, 1994.

Huntington, Roger. *Design and Development of the Indy Car*. Tucson, AZ: HP Books, 1981.

Lewis, David. *Eddie Rickenbacker, An American Hero in the Twentieth Century*. Baltimore, MD: The John Hopkins University Press, 2005.

McDonald, John P. *Lost Indianapolis*. Mount Pleasant, SC: Arcadia Publishing, 2002.

Reed, Terry. *Indy, The Race and the Ritual of the Indianapolis 500*. Dulles, VA: Brassey's, Inc., 1980.

Riggs, L. Spencer and Rick Popely. *Indianapolis 500 Chronicle*. Lincolnwood, IL: Publications International, 1998.

Scott, D. Bruce. *Indy, Racing Before The 500*. Batesville, IN: Indiana Reflections, 2005.

Shaw, Wilbur. *Gentlemen, Start Your Engines*. New York: Coward-McCann, 1955.

Taylor, Rich. *Indy, 75 Years of Racing's Greatest Spectacle*. New York: St. Martin's Press, 1991.

Wayne, Gary. *The Watson Years: When Roadsters Ruled the Speedway*. Marshall IN: Witness Prod., 2001.

INDEX

Cutlass, 170
D.A. Lubricants, 162
Dahl, Arlene, 58
Dallara, 211, 249, 250, 251
Dallenbach, Eloise "Dolly," 35, 80
dash scroll button, 195
Davis, Floyd, 76, 241
Dawson, Joe, 19, 236
Daytona International Speedway, 159
Daywalt, Jimmy, 94, 103
Dean, Al, 119
Dean Van Lines, 103
de Ferran, Gil, 206, 211, 250
de Figueiredo, Ana Beatriz Caselato Gomes
     "Bia," 153
Delage, 39, 237
Delporte, Mike, 133
Delta 88, 139
Delta Faucet, 249
DePalma, Ralph, 19, 21, 36, 40, 237
DePaolo, Peter, 40, 48, 239
DePaul University, 162
de Silvestro, Simona, 152, 153
Detroit Special, 32
Devore, Billy, 88, 241
DFX, 167
Dixon, Scott, 219, 222, 251
Dodge, 190
Domino's Pizza, 248
Donohue, Mark, 132, 135, 136, 138, 142, 216,
     245
Drake, Dale, 48, 86
Dreyer & Reinbold Racing team, 225
Duckworth, Keith, 167
Duesenberg,
     Augie, 32, 40
     brothers, 35, 40, 41
     car, 27, 30, 36, 40, 41, 51, 67, 238, 239, 239
     factory team, 40, 49
     Fred, 32, 40
Dunlop, 110
Dunn Engineering, 94
Duno, Milka, 153, 232
Durant,
     Billy, 16, 38, 240
     Cliff, 240
Duray, Leon, 28
Eagle, 129, 136, 138, 158, 245, 246
Earhart, Amelia, 160
Edwards, Anthony, 216
Elisian, Ed, 98
Epperly, David "Quin," 99
Evans, Dave, 113
Fabi, Teo, 162, 177
Fageol,
     car, 81
     Lou, 105
Fengler, Harlan, 106, 116

Ferguson, Andrew, 107
Fiat, 40
Firestone,
     company, 78
     Harvey, 160
     tires, 110
First National City Traveler's Checks, 246
Fisher,
     Carl, 11, 12, 13, 17, 19, 20, 42, 48, 73, 74, 76,
          78, 85, 106, 188, 224
     Sarah, 152, 225, 232
Fittipaldi, Emerson "Emmo," 165, 170, 181, 190,
     193, 206, 248, 249
Flaherty, Pat, 87, 89, 90, 94, 99, 243
Follmer, George, 124
Ford,
     car/engine, 52, 54, 81, 113, 115, 116, 124, 142,
          244
     company, 52, 106, 113, 167, 167
     Edsel, 52
     Henry, 160
Formula Ford, 211
Formula One, 106, 107, 112, 113, 167, 170, 181,
     186, 190, 206
Fortner, Jack, 80
Fox,
     Bill, 81
     Stan, 191
Foyt,
     A.J., 103, 110, 113, 115, 116, 117, 119, 120,
          127, 134, 136, 139, 145, 158, 180, 192,
          205, 218, 244, 246, 250
     A.J. IV, 218, 243, 246
     Larry, 244
     Power Team, 250
Frame, Fred, 50, 240
Franchitti, Dario, 219, 227, 234, 251
Frey, Don, 113
Frontenac, 36, 38, 238
fuel map switch, 195
Gable, Clark, 87, 160
Galles, Rick, 177
Galmer, 248
Ganassi, Chip, 206
Garner, James, 139
Garza, Josele, 157
General Motors, 32, 76, 168, 193, 207
George, Mari Hulman, 59, 225, 235
George, Tony, 185, 186, 188, 190, 197, 206, 219,
     220, 235, 241
Gilmore, 240, 246
Golden Anniversary, 106
Goldsmith, Paul, 115
Goodwood Festival of Speed, 132, 242, 243, 249
Goodyear, Scott, 186, 191, 193, 199
Goosen, Leo, 35, 43, 73, 123
Gould, 246
Goux, Jules, 19, 237, 238

Granatelli,
     Andy, 89, 108, 118, 119, 126, 127, 129
     Joe, 129
     Vince, 129
Grancor, 80
Grand Prix, 35, 40, 67, 71, 106, 206, 237, 238
Greco, Marco, 201
Green, Cecil, 93
Guerrero, Roberto, 157, 177, 199
Gurney, Dan, 106, 110, 111, 112, 113, 122, 136,
     158, 162
Guthrie, Janet, 145, 152
Haas, Carl, 162, 167
Hall-Barnard, 158
Hall, Jim, 154, 155, 162
Hall, Norm, 119
Hall of Fame Museum, 28, 30, 50, 60, 76, 94, 134,
     135, 236, 237, 238, 239, 240, 241, 242,
     243, 244, 245, 246, 247, 248, 249, 250
Hamilton, Ken, 173
Hanks, Sam, 99, 103, 243
Hannon, Johnny, 60
Hargitay, Mickey, 161
Harrah, Bill, 143
Harroun, Ray, 10, 13, 18, 236
Hartz, Harry, 50
Harvest Classic, 186
Hawk, 245
Hemelgarn Racing, 249
Henao, Adriana, 226
Henderson,
     Florence, 225
     Pete, 27
Henning, Henry "Cotton," 66, 75
Hepburn, Ralph, 44, 52, 56, 63, 81
Hilborn, Stu, 86, 87, 89
Hill, Graham, 119, 128, 244
Hobbs, David, 137
Holland, Bill, 79, 81, 86, 242
Holstet, 248
Honda, 207
Hope, Bob, 147
Hopkins, Lindsey, 93, 113
Horn, Ted, 52
Hornish, Sam Jr., 204, 212, 216, 224, 251
Houck, Jerry, 50
Hulman & Company, 220
Hulman, Anton, "Tony," 50, 60, 71, 72, 75, 76,
     80, 86, 93, 94, 97, 103, 139, 143, 145, 149,
     186, 188, 190, 224, 237
Hulme, Dennis, 132
Hunter-Reay, Ryan, 88, 215
Hurtubise, Jim, 123, 139, 140
Hyatt Bearings, 32
Hy-Gain, 246
Illien, Mario, 168, 192
Ilmor, 168, 187, 192, 193, 207
Ilmor/Chevy, 170, 187, 191